Biography and Reflections of a Globe Trotting Pensioner
Introducing Odyssey 2000

Arthur Benbow

January 1st 2000 to December 31st 2000

30,400 kilometers in 366 day

ENJOY READING THIS 366 DAY
CYCLE RIDE AROUND THE WORLD
RAISING £8.000 FOR THE NSPCC

BEST WISHES

Arthur Benbow
4 Applemore House,
Hilcroft Close
Lymington, Hants SO41 9BA
Tel: 07505844002
arthurbenbow21@gmail.com

AuthorHouse™ UK
1663 Liberty Drive
Bloomington, IN 47403 USA
www.authorhouse.co.uk
Phone: 0800 047 8203 (Domestic TFN)
+44 1908 723714 (International)

Published by AuthorHouse 07/31/2019

ISBN: 978-1-7283-9153-3 (sc)
ISBN: 978-1-7283-9152-6 (e)

Print information available on the last page.

This book is printed on acid-free paper.

authorHOUSE®

Arthur Benbow & UK companion John Ambler
At the finish 31st December 2000

John has kindly produced his reflections on the bike ride of a lifetime

Crazy, mad, impossible those were my first thoughts on seeing Tim Kneeland's advertisement in the cycling press. My second thought was I want to do it. It being the potential 21,000 mile cycle ride lasting 1 year that was Odyssey 2000. Unlike Arthur who endured sleepless nights deciding on whether or not to apply, for me the time was right, and I joined up immediately. I had practiced dental surgery in the same room for 30 years, and was ready to escape into the wide, wide World..I was 58 at the time and I had some experience of long distance bike rides. so I knew what I was letting myself in for.

My family were all grown up, and my wife was supportive of the idea. Celia had been less supportive of my previous idea which had been to sail a sailboat round the World, so with my pass signed I was off. This is when Arthur got in touch and we prepared and trained together. Arthur is a bundle of energy and became a true friend and this book is his view of Odyssey as we usually called it.

I have added a few comments (in italics) where I recall an incident of note, and there were plenty of those. As I said earlier it was mad and it shouldn't have worked, but it did. All credit to Tim Kneeland for making it happen and the 247 Odyssey riders who set off on the ride and who became a family. Those that made it to the end can be justly proud of what they had achieved.

———————————————————————

There is one other companion the author would like to introduce readers to that is Len Beil one of the first US riders to register who has been a great support to Arthur on further cycling projects in the UK and beyond

I am honoured to know and call Arthur my friend. I had the pleasure of meeting him on the Odyssey 2000 as we cycled around the world for a year.

I've always considered myself athletic, but didn't start riding a bicycle more than 3 miles at a time until 1984 at the age of 39. At the time, I was involved in efforts to stop smoking in the workplace and joined an American Lung Association ride through the Seattle, San Juan Island and Vancouver Island areas, organized by Tim Kneeland. It was the start of a new adventure and a way of experiencing the world we live in.

Since then, I have completed over 15 long distance rides organized by Tim Kneeland, including a Transamerica and a Pacific Coast ride. It is fair to say I became a Kneeland groupie rider and have included my wife, Stella, and family in some of the adventures. In December 1992 I received a notice that Tim was going to lead an around the world bike ride in 2000. It didn't take long to make a decision and I signed up a week later… 6 years before the ride!

Cycling the world with about 250 fellow riders on Odyssey 2000 was the trip of my life. The adventures and misadventures along our journey have created lasting memories. It isn't easy to be away from one's comforts and loved ones, but like most, I found my own community of people to be with, learn from and experience life in a way that most people will never get to. One of the most interesting, friendly and kind-hearted, was fellow rider Arthur Benbow. I became more familiar with Arthur when he led an auxiliary bike ride around his home town when we passed through on Odyssey and I learned what a local celebrity he is.

Our lives have continued to cross paths since the end of the ride in 2001 as Stella and I have visited Arthur twice in Great Britain and Ireland and he has visited us in Seattle several times in his continued travels around the world. A very special memory will always be when we joined Arthur for a two-week long 80th birthday celebration riding around Ireland and hiking in the Yorkshire Dales. Arthur has been a treasure in our lives and I so appreciate this book capturing so many wonderful memories and adventures. God bless you Arthur and your efforts to help make our world a better place to live and learn.

===

This book is in memory of my dear wife Sylvia and parents Reg and Ethel

Plus a big thank you to the many donors in the UK and around the world who have supported the following charity projects over a 25 year period

----

Nov 1994 250 mile cycle ride in Israel for the British Heart Foundation £2002 raised

----

May 1995 3789 mile cycle ride coast to coast across the USA for children's hospice in Wales £21,000 raised www.ty hafan wales

----

2000 366 days 30,400 kms world tour by cycle for the NSPCC UK arity

National Society for the Prevention of Cruelty to Children.

£8,000 raised

2003 a cycle tour in Nepal followed by an annual visit for the next eleven years, In 2005 along with other supporters we were the founder Trustees of a UK registered charity supporting education in that beautiful country see www.kasin.org.uk http://

===

1 January 2000

I woke up at four in the morning on New Year's Day 2000 to begin a cycling tour. This was a rather special tour. History was made that day in Southern California, when the largest cycling group ever, made up of 247 cyclists, set off on a bicycle trek around the world.

The tour, dubbed the Odyssey 2000, had taken seven years to plan. It would be the cycling event of the century. It would last 366 days and cover twenty-eight thousand kilometres, which included forty-five countries and five continents. I had retired six years earlier, and I had toured extensively during that time. The Odyssey 2000 would be the climax of years of personal planning and preparation.

We completed the first eight kilometres of day 1 in the glare of publicity, as only the Americans know how to do it. Being one of only two UK-registered riders was a unique and unforgettable experience.

The start of Odyssey 2000 coincided with the famous annual Tournament of Roses Parade in Pasadena, and all 247 of us had been invited to lead the parade at a steady five miles per hour. The nation's largest TV networks were due to screen the parade, starting at 8 a.m., but for reasons still unknown, our police motorcycle escort moved us off at 7.50 a.m. Despite this setback, an estimated one million spectators lined the famous Colorado Boulevard. Some of them had camped out the previous night to ensure a good spot.

John. We were glad to get moving as it was damn cold at that hour of the morning under the clear Californian skies. This was compounded by the fact that for the benefit of the television cameras we only wore cycling shirts and shorts. The spectators had spent their spare time waiting by throwing food at those on the other side. The result was a sticky road surface which made it difficult to ride slowly in formation. There was also something sharp in the mix as I soon developed a puncture in my rear tyre. However I dare not stop it would have caused chaos so I just kept riding - not easy with a flat tyre!.

When I registered for Odyssey 2000 in 1996, I did not fully appreciate that my final weeks of planning and preparation would be so traumatic and stressful. The climax of moving house and planning for a one-year absence came when I locked the door to April Cottage—my home in the Vale of Glamorgan—on 10 December 1999. I handed over my car keys the following day. I almost felt a sense of relief at that point, although there was much to do before our 5.30 a.m. departure for Gatwick Airport, so much so that I had not gotten to bed the previous night.

I had decided to avoid travelling over Christmas twelve months earlier, so I reserved accommodation for 12 December at Escondido, between San Diego and Los Angeles. At the time, I had no idea who, if anyone, would be travelling with me. In the end, there were six of us: John, a Cyclists' Touring Club (CTC) member from Lincolnshire; his wife, Celia; two of my friends; and my sister, Mary.

We touched down in San Diego at around 4.30 p.m. local time after a fifteen-hour flight, which included a stopover in Phoenix, Arizona. After hiring a car, we checked into our apartment near Escondido, just forty-five miles north of San Diego. The following day, we returned to San Diego, where John and I had to collect our global Odyssey 2000 bikes, the cost of which was included in our registration fee. As expected, the bikes required adjustments and additions, including our own saddles and pedals.

John. Actually we were lucky the bikes were still there because the shop thought they were Christmas stock and darn nearly sold them.

On Sunday, 19 December, we had a rendezvous with twelve of our Odyssey 2000 companions, who lived within driving or cycling distance of our apartment.

We arrived at the Hilton in Burbank, California, north of Los Angeles, on 30 December. We then enjoyed two days of meetings and celebrations with 240 cyclists—our companions for the next 366 days, commencing on New Year's Day.

So it was on with **Stage 1**

The first two days, we headed south along the Pacific coast, with overnight stops in Dana Point and San Diego. The first day was not a good start for me. Following the Rose Parade, we had to rearrange our luggage on the gear trucks and sort out our needs for day 1, all of which delayed our departure until 10.30 a.m. We then rode seventy-eight miles to Dana Point, where I arrived at the campsite just after dark. As I put up my tent, it started to rain. I had only had about four hours of sleep the night before, so this was not a very good start to the tour of a lifetime.

Cardiff State Beach (Encinitas, California)

On day 2, the sun was shining, and our route took us through national parks and on dedicated cycling tracks along the Pacific coast. The general public appeared to know who we

were and what we were about to do. As we passed, they offered encouraging remarks, such as "Good luck," "Bon voyage," and "Gee, I wanna join you guys."

3

We crossed the border into Mexico by mid-morning of the third day. Over the next fifteen days, we cycled the 1,628 kilometres through the Baja California Peninsula. This was my first visit to Mexico, and the level of poverty and unemployment sharply contrasted with that in the United States.

The traffic made cycling in Mexico dangerous; other UK cyclists had warned me about this hazard. A percentage of Mexican drivers appeared to have a kamikaze approach to driving. I saw several roadside shrines lining the highway. In the unlikely event that the Mexican government introduced a UK-style Ministry of Transport (MOT) examination, roughly 50 per cent of all vehicles would be taken off the road.

John. The macho Mexican truck drivers often removed their silencers (i.e. mufflers) with ear splitting results. They sounded like heavy machine gun fire but at least you could not fail to hear them coming!

During our first two days in Mexico, I was forced off the road by a passing truck which came within inches of me. Another Odyssey rider was not as lucky. He ended up in hospital with a broken leg after a hit-and-run driver knocked him off his cycle. To add insult to injury, this particular rider already had one artificial leg, and it was the good leg that was broken!

In the interest of safety, we introduced a strict riding protocol. We rode single file in small groups and only overtook when the road was clear.

Baja California, Mexico

Two items which we take for granted were in very short supply in Mexico: fresh drinking water and toilet paper. This shortage was aggravated by the arrival of 240 cyclists and support staff. With a continuous drought in the region, I could understand the lack of water, but not the lack of toilet paper. Cyclists consume an average of four litres of water per day. By the end of our third day in Mexico, one of our support vehicles had to return to the United States for fresh water.

I had mixed feelings about the logistics of travelling with such a large group. For instance, I never expected I'd have to stand in a queue for meals or a shower. But after eighteen days, I found my fears were unfounded. In fact, there was a tremendous community spirit throughout the group. We had social events and opportunities to meet different people. Daily riding companions were determined by age, ability, and personal choice. In my case, I could not have met up with two more suitable companions: John, my sole UK companion and a retired dental surgeon, and Warren, a retired doctor from Chicago. We were never alone on the road. There was always a group nearby, ready to help in the event of a problem, plus our six sag wagons.

Our route took us along the Pacific coast to Rosario and Ensenada. At this point, our itinerary guided us inland towards the mountains. While we remained on the west side of the Baja Peninsula for several days, we were not very far from the coast at any time.

The first rest day came at Catalina. After riding 750 kilometres in eight days, this was a welcome break. Although daytime temperatures were in the high thirties, it was very cold between sunset and sunrise. One morning, I found ice on my tent.

We encountered some very long climbs which took us through some remote deserts, where the landscape was dotted with weird carrot-like plants called *booms*.

John. Actually they were called Boojums Those familiar with the hunting of the Snark by Lewis Carroll will know a Boojum was a particularly dangerous form of Snark. The botanist that named these plants Boojums was clearly a Lewis Carroll fan.

There were also really cool multi-armed cacti called saguaro.

As we headed south through Colonel, El Rosario, and Catalina, our route took us to the east coast of Baja, where the coastal region was much more spectacular and rugged, with plenty of white sandy beaches.

On 17 January, we arrived at our final stop in Mexico: La Paz, the capital of Baja California. Here, we had another welcome rest day before flying to Costa Rica on 19 January, when we bade farewell to an unusual companion who had followed us for most of our 1,500 kilometres from Ensenada.

Our companion was a very cheerful sixty-five-year-old one-legged Mexican by the name of Artulio, and he was travelling the same route and distance as us on a hand-propelled tricycle, with his worldly possessions in a box at the rear. It appeared that Artulio made this journey every year to visit his nine children in La Paz. The Odyssey party was so taken by this man's cheerful attitude that the party raised a collection of over one thousand dollars to put towards a new tricycle for his future trips.

Following a relaxing day and two nights at the Hotel Marina in La Paz, Mexico, we departed at 7 a.m. and rode fifteen kilometres to the airport for the five-hour flight to San José, Costa Rica. This was the first of eighteen flights around the world during the Odyssey, a logistical challenge for the organisers of Odyssey 2000.

The two large container lorries, which housed the 250-odd luggage lockers and had been with us since day 1, were shipped to Athens. We would use them during the stage through southern Europe, from 16 March to 12 May, ending in Lisbon. In the meantime, similar vehicles awaited our arrival in South Africa on 13 February. For the remainder of the South American stage, we would use local trucks.

The flight south-east to Costa Rica took us into another time zone and a warmer climate. After days of cycling in the dry, dusty deserts of Mexico, we were now in the lush tropical rainforest of Latin America.

Costa Rica

With only four days in Costa Rica, my impressions during that short stay prompted me to add this area to my list of places to return to one day. It appears to be one of the most stable regions of Central America (economically and politically). The indigenous population numbers twenty-two million people, and it has a further fifty thousand residents from the USA, plus an eight-month tourist season, the attractions being both the low cost of living and the sunshine. It is also one of the most volcanic regions in the world, with over eighty volcanoes (six of them active). Our short visit's itinerary did not take us near either coastline—the Pacific one stretches for 700 miles, whilst the Caribbean coast covers only 140 miles.

Following a rest day in the capital, San José, we were set for a hard day's ride 165 kilometres to San Isidro. This distance would not normally have presented a problem for the average fit cyclist, assuming the terrain and weather were normal. Unfortunately, neither the terrain nor the weather was normal on day 22. The first thirteen kilometres out of the city took an hour of riding through the morning rush hour. Plus the route guide for that day indicated that we had a long climb ahead. We did not need the route guide to tell us that; we could see it in the distance.

We shortly started a climb which continued for seventy-nine kilometres to the summit at 3,491 metres (11,171 feet). Under good weather conditions, this ride would have been a challenge for many fit cyclists, but from the start, we were riding into a headwind and heavy rain, with the temperature getting lower as we climbed.

In the end, day 22 turned out to be one of the longest, wettest, and coldest days we had tackled since we started. In view of the short daylight hours (dark by 5.30 p.m.), many of the 240 riders were unable to make it to camp before nightfall. I personally hit a patch of oil on a hairpin bend and took a tumble. Having completed the climb, I now had a long descent to the camp at San Isidro. However, it was dark, and I was very wet and cold and feeling shaken up from the fall. In this situation, all available sag wagons were put into action to ferry the many riders who had gotten stranded on the mountain in the dark. I was advised to stay put until a vehicle could pick me up, but it was almost an hour before my lift arrived. I think that was the nearest I have ever gotten to hypothermia.

John. Me too Arthur. I was riding with Warren who lived and trained in Florida, and consequently was not at his best on hills. In the end we hitched a lift in the back of a pickup truck. The wind chill on our wet clothing nearly finished us off. I was struck by the sheer irony of the situation. To be suffering from hypothermia in the tropics was not something I had anticipated.

Fortunately, the weather improved over the remaining four days in Costa Rica with our final overnight stop in San Vito (elevation 990 metres). On day 24, we left San Vito for another twenty-five kilometres of climbing, followed by a long descent with some spectacular views. And then we headed for the border with Panama, where we had been warned to expect some delays.

Bureaucracy in Latin America moves very slowly, and the border crossing from Costa Rica into Panama was no exception. The volume of commercial and private vehicles, plus many pedestrians moving in both directions, created a very busy daily situation. However, the authorities at both crossings were totally unprepared for the arrival of over 240 cyclists, plus all the support vehicles.

John. It was late afternoon before I got through, and it was getting dark. We had to.hitch a lift to Panama City. Even today I console myself with airport delays by thinking at least it isn't as bad as Panama.

For me, moving through the first queue to exit Costa Rica, which cost five colones, took one hour. We then had one hundred yards to Panama immigration and customs, where we were sent. There, my passport was stamped at window number 1, and I was told I was free to proceed.

This puzzled me somewhat, as all my American companions were obliged to stand in another very long queue and complete an entry permit costing five dollars. I thought what applied to them must also apply to me, but my assumption was incorrect, as after standing in the queue for over forty minutes, I was again told that I was free to proceed.

So why was I getting this special treatment? It then dawned on me that the sole reason was that I held a British passport. I later learned that my companions were kept waiting for over three hours, during which time officials took it in turn to go for lunch. This incident was repeated at other border crossings in South America—an indication of Uncle Sam's popularity in the region?

Panama Canal 24th to 28th January

With no volcanic mountains to climb, our few days in Panama were a lot easier than our time in Costa Rica. Panama City was our final destination in Central America, with two nights and one and a half days for sightseeing.

The canal, completed around 1914 by the USA (with Chinese labour), helped put Panama on the world shipping map. Over one hundred major banks, together with many fine hotels, are based in Panama City. All of this brings me to stage 3.

On day 29, the six-hour flight from Panama City to Santiago, which took us over the equator, proved to be the first logistical challenge that the airline and tour organiser could not meet. Either the plane (a Lockheed L-1011) was not big enough for us, or we had too many bicycles and too much luggage. It was only after a five-hour wait in the airport departure lounge that we eventually took off for Chile with seventy-nine bikes (including mine), plus some of the support luggage left on the runway in Panama.

Arising from this, our itinerary in Santiago was extended from one to three nights to allow the missing bikes and luggage to catch up with us. Fortunately, Santiago is a very large and bustling city of over five million people, so we had plenty to see and do in the area. This extension was welcome in one respect but something we would have to pay for later.

Santiago, Chile

On day 33 (and two days behind schedule), we were reunited with our missing bikes and luggage, and we were now due to head south out of Santiago. However, getting out of Santiago during the morning rush hour had all the hallmarks of a cyclist's nightmare, in spite of the detailed instructions on our route sheet for that day. Thanks to our Chilean-born travelling doctor, Raphael, we were honoured with a motorcycle police escort out of the city.

On this occasion, it was in every rider's interest to ensure that we set off at the same time. This created a memorable scene, with many hundreds of cheering commuters (plus local TV cameras) lining the streets as 240 cyclists filed out of the hotel in the centre of Santiago with traffic held up in both directions. With our police escort, we went through red traffic lights. With traffic held up at each junction, we moved out of town and were safely escorted to the city boundary.

John. Great experience, with all the roads closed we just swept along Tour de France style

Due to the extra two days in Santiago, we now faced twelve days of riding without a break so we could catch up with this stage's itinerary. It was just as well that our route for the next few days took us through a fairly flat plateau with snow-capped mountains on either side. Overnight stops during this section included San Fernando, Talca, Cauquenes, and Concepcion, where we arrived back on the Pacific coast to a much colder climate and periodic rain.

John One night it rained so hard that instead of camping we were accommodated in a university sports hall. Throughout the night the wind howled like a demented banshee was trying to dismantle the place. We were well into Patagonia by then so it wasn't too surprising I suppose.

Around this period, yours truly (or my digestive system) decided to violently disagree with something I ate or drank. As a result, I ate very little for two days and became too weak to cycle. Then, I was pleased by and grateful for the comfort of the sag wagon, a facility I had previously declared was for wimps and invalids.

It got colder as we progressed south. The last two days (41 and 42) in Chile proved to be, as expected, some of this stage's toughest. They included climbing over the Andes to an elevation of 1,308 metres, with the weather fluctuating between warm sunshine and prolonged showers, which got colder as we got nearer to the summit. The reward for our efforts was some spectacular scenery. And around mid-afternoon on day 43 (12 February), I crossed the border into Argentina to be welcomed by warm sunshine.

We still had fifty kilometres till our first overnight stop in Argentina at Villa La Angostura, and whilst the sunshine and the descent were welcome, we now had to contend with over thirty kilometres of gravel road.

John. Some of the gravel was more like small rocks in places it was nearly unridable. In fact I fell off, though fortunately without injury. That's just as well as I don't bounce as well as I used to do.

The second day in Argentina and our last day of riding in South America, we had a mere eighty-nine kilometres to the beautiful lakeside mountain resort of San Carlos de Bariloche. Most of our route that day took us along the edge of the beautiful Lago Nahuel Huapi, with snow-capped mountains in the distance and all around. It was a spot that one could comfortably spend a few days, but within twenty-four hours, we were due to fly to Johannesburg and start the next stage.

John. The departure from from Bariloche was actually quite hairy. The only aircraft that would take us all including the bikes was a Boeing 747, but apparently the runway was just not long enough to handle a 747. To overcome this problem the plane was only partially fuelled and to take off the engines were run up to full power but with the brakes full on. When the brake were released the fully laden 747 took off down the runway like the proverbial scalded cat. The acceleration was tremendous and the cabin erupted with whoops and cries of 'Burn rubber man!'. We were quickly airborne but soon landed again at Buenos Aries to refuel to fly to South Africa

Now, my watch indicates it is 4 a.m. on 15 February, and we have just had breakfast. We are in midair, heading for Johannesburg, South Africa, where I hope to complete and dispatch this email.

Our Boeing 747 flight to South Africa took off from San Carlos de Bariloche at 17.25 last evening. This was the largest aircraft to take off from this airport in recent years. We then touched down for refuelling at Buenos Aires at 19.00, and the remainder of the flight is expected to take around nine hours, when we will be two hours ahead of Greenwich Mean Time.

It is now 21.20 local time in Johannesburg, and I am pleased to confirm that we touched down safely at around noon today. Weather here is overcast and wet underfoot from heavy rain. Unfortunately, yours truly had a delay of over three hours at the airport and will have another in the morning. It appears that I left my pedals in Argentina (so don't cry for me, Argentina). Hopefully, I will pick up a pair in the morning; I will keep you informed. With the end of stage 3, I will next report on South Africa.

We were greeted at Johannesburg Airport in South Africa with news of a very heavy depression. Three weeks of heavy storms had resulted in flooding in many areas. Fortunately, it was not raining on our arrival, just very wet underfoot. However, yours truly had a major problem in getting mobile, as prior to our flight's departure, we had needed to prepare all cycles for the plane by turning the handlebars round and removing the pedals. My problem was that my pedals, which should have been in my carry-on luggage, were not there.

After going through my bags twice, it gradually dawned on me that the pedals could only be at the campsite in Argentina, where I had removed them. Seeing all my companions cycle away from the airport for the six-kilometre ride to our hotel, I was destined for a three-hour wait until one of the tour support vehicles was available to give me a lift.

Two days later, I was able to get to a bike shop to buy new pedals, and in the meantime, I had borrowed a pair from the tour mechanic. Seven days later, the missing pedals turned up in the lost-and-found box in our support van. It appeared that a staff member had picked them up before our final departure from the campground in Argentina. So I now had a spare pair of pedals in my luggage and would not make that mistake again.

Oribi Gorge

Let me say that when we first arrived in South Africa, I sensed almost a touch of nostalgia in the air; it felt just like home. First of all, we were able to cycle on the *right* side of the road (sorry, the left). Then, I was able to enjoy my first decent cup of tea since December. Plus, almost everyone here spoke English, and finally, it was raining.

Plettenberg Bay

The first twelve days in South Africa were hectic and traumatic, to say the least, and would not be forgotten by me or any of my companions. Prior to our arrival in South Africa, a cyclone coming in from the Indian Ocean had battered Mozambique and the surrounding regions. This had a major effect on Odyssey 2000, but more on that problem later.

The day we arrived in Johannesburg was down on the itinerary as a rest day. But there was very little time for R & R, as I did not arrive at the hotel till 5 p.m., and the next day, day 47, we were off to Middelburg, a distance of 154 kilometres. Whilst the rain kept off for the next two days, we were riding into increasingly strong winds, and by the time we arrived at Hazyview three days later, we were ready for another layover day.

Lunch stop en route to Middelburg (Day 47)

Prior to our departure from England, my sole UK companion, John, and I had made a reservation for a two-day safari at Kruger National Park, which was a three-hour drive from our hotel at Hazyview. It appeared that many other Odyssey riders had done likewise, but no one had anticipated the damage that the heavy storms and subsequent flooding had caused. Due to bridges being washed away and roads underwater, our safari had to move to another location in the park. Fortunately, this was not a major problem, considering the size of Kruger National Park (equal to the size of Wales).

Our late evening and early morning safari was designed to enable us to see the many animals, some of them nocturnal, in natural surroundings, from elephants to tigers, giraffes to impalas. Speaking of the impala, I would like to reproduce something which caught my eye whilst in the park, as follows.

Every morning in Africa an impala wakes up, she knows that she has to run faster than the lion or die. Every morning in Africa a lion wakes up, he knows that he has to run faster than the impala or starve. In fact, no matter who you are, when the sun comes up in Africa, you had better start running.

The daily route guides had warned us that our itinerary in South Africa would cover some pretty demanding terrain but that it also included some of the most beautiful country in the world. It promised to be hot, remote, and mostly rural without too many full-service areas. Many of the country roads do not have a shoulder and can be quite busy.

So this was our advance warning of what to expect; in reality, we encountered the unexpected knock-on effect of the recent cyclone coming in from the Indian Ocean and hitting Africa in general and Mozambique in particular. Added to this, we had the warning of the high level of crime, including muggings and even hijackings. It was, in fact, inadvisable to walk the streets of any large town alone.

Following our safari and two-day break at Hazyview, the itinerary took us for two days into Swaziland, where we were due to arrive on day 53 prior to a five-day ride to Durban. However, on day 54, seventy-five Odyssey riders, including yours truly, found themselves in Durban.

Durban is a beautiful city on the Indian Ocean that has many clean beaches, which makes it a popular holiday destination. In spite of the apparent prosperity, it still has much poverty and unemployment. Personally, I think that politicians need to review their priorities when eight- to ten-year-old children are sleeping on the streets at ten in the morning.

So why did we arrive in Durban late on Wednesday night when we were not due till Saturday? Good question. Well, on day 53 (Tuesday), after 703 of the most demanding kilometres in South Africa, we arrived for our two days in Swaziland; that particular day was 169 kilometres. Ever since leaving Johannesburg, we had been buffeted by strong headwinds and periodic storms, and temps in the high nineties in between. This was the edge of the cyclone which had been battering Mozambique. And Tuesday (day 53) was a very hot and hilly day, with two mountain passes over six thousand feet, and yours truly (along with many others) felt a trifle stretched to the limit at the end of that day. The final straw that broke the camel's back was a heavy storm that occurred as yours truly was trying to put up his tent in the dark—the outcome being that the tent was so wet inside and out, I had to sleep with others on the campsite's washroom floor. The next morning, it was still raining heavily and looked set to do so for the day.

Basically, I was now at the Durban Holiday Inn overlooking the Indian Ocean, enjoying a few days of R & R, because morale had gotten so low among a lot of Odyssey folk. By Tuesday, seventy-five of us had hired two coaches to transport us, plus bikes and luggage, for the nine-hour drive down to Durban. (The cost worked out to approximately sixteen pounds each and was well worth it.) As you can imagine, with seventy-five bikes and luggage, it took nearly two hours to load the coaches. So with another hour spent at the border getting back into South Africa, plus getting food for the journey, we eventually arrived at Durban around 10 p.m. Luckily, it was out of season here, so most of us got into the Holiday Inn, and the cost for three people sharing a room was a massive ten pounds per night and well worth it.

John. We arrived in Durban late at night only to find the hotel we intended to use was in a doubtful area which none of us felt comfortable about. Consequently all 75 of us moved to better hotels. As it was nearly midnight by then I was amazed that we were able to do that. Try this in London and you wouldn't be so lucky.

This break gave us an opportunity to catch up on washing, writing correspondence, and replacing numerous items on the bikes, which were showing signs of wear after nearly five thousand k

Another ongoing problem which was of some concern among our party was the very high crime rate in this part of South Africa. Here, we were advised not to travel alone, and muggings happened regularly. Two of our party were involved in two separate incidents. Fortunately, no one suffered any injury or loss of personal items.

Having said that, the Odyssey party received tremendous welcomes at almost every town and community we visited, not just in Africa but from Costa Rica to Chile. Young children in particular stood in large groups, cheering and clapping. There had been concerts and dancing displays laid on during or after supper. In Dullstroom, South Africa, for instance, a newspaper report on our visit went as follows: ("Odyssey cycles into town.")

It was a misty Thursday, 17 February, when Odyssey 2000 cyclists trickled into Dullstroom—a month and a half and 4,500 kilometres into their yearlong cycling expedition around the world. The first to arrive was nineteen-year-old True Brown from Vermont, soon followed by three hundred cyclists, aged between eighteen and eighty, and their vast support team.

John. Ar Dullstroom the children welcoming us were mostly wearing wellington boots but that didn't stop their dance routine. On the other hand the heavy drizzle reminiscent of Scotland deterred us from camping in the waterlogged campsite. In the circumstances the attraction of the local inn which would not have looked out of place in England was overwhelming and we hastened there to escape the rain and revive both body and spirit.

From the supper queue at the Dullstroom Inn came many a jovial remark: "The people in—where are we?—South Africa are very hospitable. We took a wrong turn coming out of Johannesburg and were waved back on track by supporters. At our first checkpoint, a local farmer was handing out free Cokes to all of us."

The group were welcomed by singing children from the community and Dullstroom's mayor, Mr Isaac Mthombeni. They were heading for Hazyview and the Lowveld. Saturday, we would transfer to another hotel three blocks away, where Odyssey was booked for two nights, and await the rest of the crowd who were, no doubt, still struggling with the elements. Then on Monday, we would commence the sixteen-day trek down to Cape Town; at least that was the official itinerary.

However, the official itinerary for that period did not leave any spare time for sightseeing, with only one rest day plus one day off in Cape Town before flying to Athens. Some of us felt that a short break from Odyssey was advisable. A combination of factors prompted this idea. Firstly, there were the uncertain weather conditions. Then, we heard about the Cape Argus cycle event due to take place in Cape Town on Sunday, 13 March, which was two days before the Odyssey party's arrival.

Camps Bay, Cape Town

We also discussed the press report of record rainfall in Port Elizabeth (on our route to Cape Town); the rainfall for January and February had been equal to half the annual average. Many streets were flooded, and motorists were asked to exercise caution. Then we had to consider the advice that from Port Elizabeth onwards, in particular along the Garden Route to Cape Town, there was much to see and do. With only one rest day in Cape Town on 15

March, the official itinerary did not leave any spare time for sightseeing. So a number of Odyssey riders, including yours truly, agreed to go off route and do our own thing for the next two weeks.

Plus, on Sunday, 12 March, some of us were interested in taking part in the very big bike event in Cape Town. This event (classed as a race but more like a major audax-cum-charity ride), known as the Cape Argus Cycle Tour, takes in a very scenic and hilly 109-kilometre route around the Cape Peninsula. It has a time limit of six and a half hours.

Waterfront Cape Town

There had been some doubt as to whether we were too late to officially ride. We were advised that entries closed on January 14 or once thirty-five thousand entries had been taken. However, thanks to a local cycling club, we were assured at least three places. We later heard that approximately twenty Odyssey riders had been accepted.

According to the local press, the Cape Argus Cycle Tour is one of the largest amateur sporting events in the world, and in 1999, the event attracted over thirty thousand riders from all over the country and beyond. In the end, approximately fifty Odyssey folk rode the 110-kilometre Cape Argus Cycle Tour race along with thirty-five thousand other folk, including quite a number of international riders, several from the UK. Whilst I did not see him in person, I understand that CTC president Phil Liggett also did the ride, as he had been there to commentate on the five-day Giro del Capo professional race, which had finished in Cape Town on Saturday.

A number of the riders in the pro event rode on Sunday by invitation, starting at 6 a.m. They were followed by all the seeded riders, and from 8 a.m., the remaining riders were dispatched in groups every four minutes. Every individual rider was timed with a transponder fitted to the right ankle, and whilst I do not have yours truly's official time, my estimate would be around 4 hours and 30 minutes.

This event covers some fantastic scenery, although there was a route change from previous years because of a rockfall on Chapman's Peak, which had killed a local man a few months before. I understand that there were around 1,416 metres of climbing in total, and an estimated two hundred thousand spectators were around the course, including jazz bands and scantily dressed dancing girls. I can't think of why, but several Odyssey riders suggested we make this event an annual reunion. I, for one, will be back next year, 2001

John. The Cape Argus ride was a huge morale booster for us. Until then we had not been riding against other riders, and now we realised just how super-fit we had become. Other riders on light weight bikes were surprised that we had laden ourselves with cameras, various bags, etc. and were finding it an easy ride, the sort of thing we did every day on Odyssey. On one hill in the noonday heat several riders collapsed and were resuscitated with oxygen. Apparently there have been deaths on the ride in the past.

v The Cape Argus charity ride in Cape Town (thirty-three thousand participants)

After the event, one news item caused us to laugh. It is a fact that much of this ride takes place in a national park on the Cape Peninsula. At several points, you can see a warning to the public (not seen in the UK) to *not* feed the baboons. The news item said that on one stretch of the route, baboons were trying to cross the road but could not because of a continual stream of cyclists. The baboons, I understand, ended up throwing banana skins at the peloton.

Major distraction on the Cape Argus charity ride

So this was a fitting climax to our final two weeks in South Africa. It really is a beautiful country, with Cape Town and the surrounding area as the jewel in the crown—an area which I hope to return to for further exploration.

On day 75, 15 March, with a total of 7,317 kilometres completed, the Odyssey cavalcade assembled at Cape Town International Airport for the night flight to Athens to start stage 5. This next stage would take us from Athens to Barcelona. It would last for forty-four days and would be the longest yet.

My next report will contain a response to the many email enquiries which I have had from folk who would like to know more about Odyssey, what attracts folk to give up a whole year of their lives, and whether there will be another one.

According to our route sheet for day 92, we were now almost exactly 25 per cent into our global trek. And having covered 1,656 kilometres in stage 5 and 9,008 kilometres since 1 January, I had come to the conclusion that this trip was not for the faint-hearted or for wimps. Having said that, I had no regrets and knew I would come out of this with a wide circle of friends. And maybe a little wiser and fitter?

As I indicated in my previous report on stage 4 from South Africa, stage 5 in Mediterranean Europe is Odyssey's longest stage, covering forty-four days from Athens to Barcelona. Just in case anyone out there should have forgotten who this globe-trotting pensioner was during that period, I thought it best to split that stage into two reports.

Athens

Herewith, I will reflect on Odyssey 2000's twenty-two-day period from Athens to Assisi, Italy, a distance of 1,887 kilometres, as promised in my last report and in response to a number of email enquiries which I have had since we started. Plus, I want to respond to the considerable interest and (some envy) that UK cyclists I came into contact with expressed prior to the start of Odyssey 2000. I will at this stage explain a little about the daily life of an Odyssey 2000 cyclist, and what could prompt anyone to give up a year of his or her life in order to ride a bicycle around the world.

The average age of the 240-strong party is forty-nine, with the youngest clocking in at nineteen years of age and the eldest at seventy-nine. The majority live in the USA, but there are also contingents from Canada, France, Switzerland, Chile, and Sri Lanka, with just two cyclists from the UK. Many folk who have not yet reached retiring age will be looking for new jobs when they return to normal life. Some have sold their houses and cars; some have just let their houses.

When one recently retired couple informed their family of their plans for the millennium, their family responded, "Why can't you be like other folk and buy a motorhome?" Then, there are two couples who are spending their honeymoon on the trip.

Tim Kneeland & associates have been in the bike tour business since the early eighties and has a good reputation among American and UK cyclists. Odyssey 2000 was in the planning for seven years, and the next one is proposed for the year 2003, possibly with a smaller group.

Each rider has a 17-inch-square, 36-inch-deep personal locker in a specially designed gear truck; this has to accommodate all your luggage and camping gear. In addition, there are over a dozen support vehicles, mobile showers, and sag wagons all in radio contact, with a support crew of nearly thirty. This includes three qualified masseurs. Every rider is entitled to one free massage every three weeks; you have to pay for any further massage in that period.

Two vehicles and technical staff are responsible for all service and repairs to the top-of-the-range US Raleigh touring bike issued to every rider before the start and included in the tour's costs. We do have to pay for new tyres and any routine replacements. Several couples have tandems, and they have to make their own provisions for replacements, spares, and so on.

We are camping for 40 per cent of the trip with two rest or travel days per week. If the campsite we use does not have adequate showers, then we have the mobile showers, which can be erected within an hour. Two things the tour organiser considers essential for any biker on a trip of this nature are hot showers and two good meals a day, which we do get most of the time. Breakfast is usually available from 6.30 to 8 a.m., and when you are camping, this means getting up around 5.30 a.m. When we have a long day, I am usually on the road at 7 for 7.30 a.m.

A DRG is issued at breakfast every morning. We average just under eighty miles per day, and at the end of some days, when you get to camp, by the time you have had a shower, put up your tent, and had supper, you are ready for

There are always checkpoints halfway through and at the end of each day to account for every rider. If any rider has mechanical problems, is taken ill, or is on the road after nightfall, then the sag wagon picks up him or her. Temporary staff are taken on as drivers and such for each country we visit; this also helps when we are not in an English-speaking country. We will have around eighteen flights between countries, several ferries, and a couple of train journeys.

People in the 240-strong party have a wide range of riding abilities. A large number of experienced and strong riders came well prepared for the twelve months ahead. Some have found the experience more than they had expected, resulting in days off the bike. In the first three months, there have been six serious accidents resulting in hospital treatment and possible repatriation.

The youngest rider, at nineteen years of age, appears to be on the brink of a promising racing career. Watch for the name of True (Trueheart) Brown. I understand that True gave up an invitation to spend the summer at the USA's Olympic training village in order to cycle the world with Odyssey 2000. True will often arrive at camp before the gear trucks, and on one day in South Africa, I happened to be at camp when True arrived, looking very fresh after a hilly ride of 177 kilometres at an average speed of thirty-five kilometres per hour. Anyone who would like more information can check out this website. **http://www.arthursmemoirs.co.uk** created in Wales by cycling friend Paul Jones who registered the website in 2001 and sadly died a few years later

So back to stage 5, which started with our flight from Cape Town to Athens. This flight was scheduled for 10 p.m. on 16 March, and our instructions were to arrive at the airport by 5 p.m. for loading the bikes and baggage. What had not been confirmed was the fact that we were to fly with the same plane (a Boeing 747) and flight crew that had taken us from Argentina to South Africa five weeks before. This was good news to all the Odyssey party, who were personally welcomed on board by the captain and owner, Prince Ahmed.

We eventually took off just after midnight, with supper served an hour later to a rather tired bunch of bikers. The flight was, as scheduled, almost exactly ten hours, touching down at Athens around 10.30 a.m. on 17 March.

An unforeseen problem awaited us as we collected our luggage and bikes at Athens Airport. It appeared that the Odyssey gear trucks containing our luggage lockers, which had been shipped from Mexico back in January, could not be released by the Greek customs and excise for some reason. This resulted in us hiring local trucks at short notice so we could transfer all the luggage to our hotel. This meant another delay, as no one could leave the airport until we had accounted for all the luggage and transferred it to our hotel. The day of our arrival, 17 March, was down on the itinerary as a rest day (much needed after a night flight). In the end, and after a fifteen-kilometre ride from the airport, we checked in at the Astir Palace Hotel between 5 and 6 p.m.

Approximately twelve hours later, on day 78, breakfast was served to 240 rather tired bikers who were about to commence a mere 144-kilometre ride out of Athens and along the coast to New Epidavros. Our DRG for that day ran to three pages, with one and a half devoted to our passage through and out of Athens. Anyone who has cycled in Athens will know that 7 to 9 a.m. is a busy time on the streets, plus the fact that Greek drivers in general, and those in Athens in particular, appear to use the car accelerator and the horn to maximum effect.

The temperature noticeably dropped between Cape Town and Athens, which meant digging out the leg and arm warmers and having rain gear at hand. After 11 a.m., we stopped for coffee and pastries, feeling just a little fragile after having exited Athens in one piece and glad to be in the country.

Our route for the rest of the day included a few climbs along the coast, where the scenery improved with every kilometre. It also took us over the famous Corinth Canal via a narrow wooden bridge, which was very slippery in spite of the fact that it was a warm, sunny day. Further investigation confirmed why it was wet. In order to allow shipping to pass through, the bridge was lowered to the canal bed. As we crossed the bridge (in single file and on foot), I heard someone with an American accent declare behind me, "You know, construction of this canal was started by the Romans."

"Yes," came a response (in an English accent). "And it was finished by Wimpey Ltd."

The first campsite at New Epidavros was right on the coast, and as camping in Southern Europe was not yet under way, this site was opened up for our party's overnight stay. Day 2 took us to (Tiros, Arcadia), a pleasant route with abundant olive and orange trees. The route that day also took us through the town of Nafplio, the first capital of Greece.

The itinerary on day 80 took us inland and towards the mountains, which were not looking very inviting with low clouds and snow in the distance. At twenty-three kilometres, we began a climb which continued for the next twenty-nine kilometres. This 1,200-metre climb was interrupted by a visit to the Elonis Monastery, built at a very high point on the cliff face. It was then a question of putting on warm clothing for the long descent to our overnight stop at Sparta.

.Day 81 started with another long climb of 1,370 metres into the mountains and down to Gialova, which took us back to the coast. However, the weather was not in our favour today, as within fifteen kilometres, we were climbing into rain which turned to snow as we got higher. Feeling very wet and cold, we arrived at the summit and to a very welcome respite at a restaurant with a roaring log fire. After the warm-up and food, we now faced a long and fast descent with many sharp 180-degree curves. By the end of the day, there were three reported accidents, with riders coming to grief on the descent.

John. On this long descent it was necessary to hang onto the brake levers quite a lot of the time. This became increasingly difficult as my hands felt as if they were turning into blocks of ice. It was a question of whether I would get to the bottom before frost-bite set in or not. At least it certainly felt that way.

The last of our six days in Greece took us to Olympia, where the Olympics began. With a population of less than one thousand, Olympia is a popular tourist area with plenty of places to eat and explore. Whilst we made time to eat, we had no time left for exploring, as our last day in Greece required an early start. So on day 83, in 2°C weather, we were on the road at 7 a.m. for the 135-kilometre ride to the port of Patras.

We had to arrive at Patras before 4 p.m. in order to catch our first cruise ferry to Italy. This was an overnight crossing, so we had bunks, supper, and breakfast all provided in reasonable comfort before our docking at Bari, on Italy's south-east coast, around 8 a.m. on day 84.

On our first day in Italy, we had a comparatively short ride of sixty-seven kilometres to Alberobello. However, Bari is a fairly large and busy port, so the sudden appearance of 240-odd cyclists at 8.30 a.m. did cause some confusion in an already-busy thoroughfare. We had gone no more than one kilometre from the harbour when the column of Odyssey riders suddenly came to a halt.

Several minutes passed before word came back along the line that the reason for our delay was that the local carabinieres were awaiting instructions from the higher authority as to what they should do about (or with) these invading bikers who were adding to the morning rush-hour confusion. A jovial comment passed back along the line that ending up in jail would at least give us a room and a hot shower for the night. We eventually started to move with the approval and direct support of the motorcycle traffic police, who safely escorted the column of bikers out of town.

John. That was the theory of it. The motor cycle policeman I was following along with a large number of other riders led us through a housing estate where he somehow lost us. Soon there were riders heading in all directions and some going round in circles. Eventually we sorted ourselves out with somewhat less faith in the Italian police. The previous occasion we rode behind a police escort in Chile worked much better. To be fair the Bari police did lay on an escort at a moment's notice and no planning. It was still very welcome.

Our second day in Italy took us to Lido di Metaponto at the southernmost tip of Italy before our trek north and up the west coast. The first welcome rest day since leaving Cape Town occurred on day 86, when we were able to explore Scalea, a coastal resort with an old town.

The itinerary now followed the west coast north through the historic town of Paestum, which has the archaeological site of a Greek city (pre-Roman Empire). This was followed by one of the most spectacular coastal rides which one could wish to have on a cycle. I refer to the Amalfi Coast, which winds its way around bay after bay with long, steady climbs followed by equally long descents.

Amalfi Coast (Italy)

Some light relief came on day 90 towards the end of a very good ride to Pompeii. When we had to negotiate the afternoon rush hour of Naples, a small Pekingese dog was spotted crossing the busy road with a pair of ladies' underwear in its mouth. Several gallant male members in the party offered to set up a search party to find the owner. I'm not quite sure whether they wanted to assist the owner of the dog or the owner of the underwear.

An overnight stop at Pompeii, from which our campsite was just across the road, made it possible to visit this famous historic city's archaeological remains. It was on 24 August 79 AD that the coastal city of Pompeii, with a population of eight to ten thousand, was obliterated with the black river of ash which came from Mount Vesuvius's summit. The population at the time of the eruption consisted of 60 per cent free men and 40 per cent slaves. It takes a good three hours to wander through the city's remains, so having a guide is advantageous.

An amusing incident arose during our tour of Pompeii (and was recorded on film). One male member of the Odyssey party was seen coming out of a brothel with a smile on his face. Unfortunately for him, the premises had closed down nearly two thousand years prior, with the anger of Mount Vesuvius.

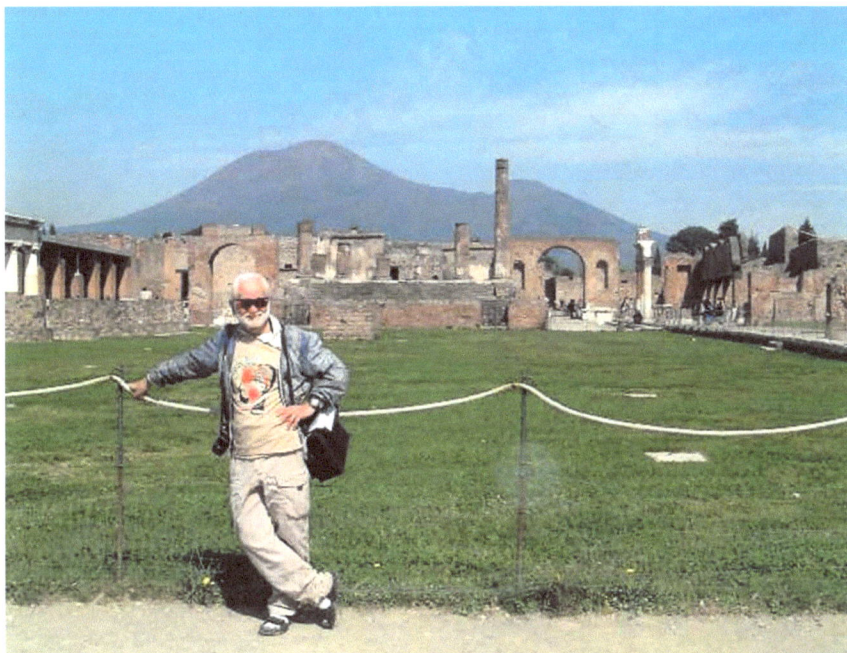

On day 93, we arrived for two days in the world's Eternal City, Rome, which could be described as an open-air museum. The guidebooks tell you that people have been building roads in and around Rome for nearly 2,500 years, and personally, I think it is about time they stopped. Any tourist arriving in Rome for the first time usually gets lost in the maze of one-way streets. So it was lucky that our campsite, from which we had a good public transport system, was ten kilometres from the city centre. I have to admit that I found walking around this beautiful city to be more tiring than a 150-kilometre cycle ride. From the Colosseum to the Parthenon, the Piazza Navona, and finally Vatican City, we really could only scratch the surface in the day and a half at our disposal.

St Peter's Cathedral (Vatican City)

From Rome, our itinerary took us 160 kilometres to Assisi for another rest day. Here, we were housed at a very comfortable hotel managed and run by Franciscan monks. Assisi I found to be a fascinating town with a tremendous history, but much quieter than Rome.

John. My mental image of a monk as being somewhat withdrawn from the World was dealt a blow when I saw them walking around the cloisters with mobile phones clamped to their ears, and following that had to struggle to reach the bar through all the monks propping it up.

Well, after a rest day in Assisi, we have just six days left in Italy, which will take us to Urbino, Florence, Pisa, and Genoa before heading into the South of France en route to Barcelona. All of this, I think, must come with my next report, which will cover the remainder of stage 5 from Assisi to Barcelona.

Assisi to Barcelona

We departed from Assisi on day 98 for the 108-kilometre ride to Urbino (birthplace of Raphael). This was a punishing day, with two mountain climbs equal to an elevation of nine thousand feet. The effort was rewarded with some magnificent views.

John. We knew by now that when the word 'scenic' appeared in the Daily Route Guide (DRG) that this meant hills, usually big hills. This was definitely a scenic ride, and a pretty tough one at that. In Italy the campsite or hotel was invariably on a mountain peak so that meant a tough climb to finish the day.

Days 99 to 102 took us to Caprese Michelangelo, Florence, and Pisa. The terrain was now not so hilly. Yours truly will remember the ride from Florence to Pisa for the rain that continued for most of the day and my rear tyre that blew out just eight kilometres from town. The route from Pisa took to the hills again with a vengeance, stopping at Levanto, a cool historic town on the coast, and Genoa. We were again rewarded for the climbing with some superb coastal scenery.

John. It was at this point our gear trucks are impounded because of a problem with insurance. This meant a couple of days wearing the same cycling gear as we temporarily lost contact with our kit. With no sleeping bags we had to be accommodated in hotels. The Odyssey staff cut the locks on the gear-trucks and we were eventually reunited with our kit. By this time as a group we had acquired a distinct odour. In a hotel lift I noticed a lady holding her nose to block the aroma emanating from our unwashed cycle clothing.

France 14ᵗʰ April to 23ʳᵈ April

Day 105 saw the end of our ride through Italy and into the South of France. Following two rest days in Nice, we headed west through St-Tropez and along the Mediterranean Coast, passing the homes of the rich and famous. Luckily for us, the tourist season was not in full swing.

Day 114 saw the start of the Pyrenees from Carcassonne to Ax-les-Thermes (110 kilometres). This was one of those days which would not be forgotten in a hurry—not so much for the climbs, spread over 90 kilometres to the summit at 1,431 metres (4,579 feet), or the spectacular views en route, which were some consolation.

Following a hard day's climbing, the steep and curvy descent into the mountain resort of Ax-les-Thermes lasted for only 10.5 kilometres. We were due to camp that night, a prospect I did not relish. Fortunately, one of my companions who had arrived ahead of me booked a room at one of the town's hotels, all of which were in great demand that night.

Day 115 was our last day in France and the Pyrenees; on paper, it was down as an eighty-two-kilometre ride. Closer examination of the day's route sheet indicated that the first thirty-six kilometres, we would be climbing (again) to the crest of the Pyrenees at 2,407 metres (7,702 feet). Fortunately, the weather had much improved since the previous day, which enabled us to appreciate the climb (covered by the '98 Tour de France) and subsequent views from the snow-capped summit.

John. The ski slopes were now below us!

Here, we took a breather and some refreshment before starting a descent which lasted for almost forty-six kilometres, taking us through Andorra and to our first campsite in Spain at La Seu d'Urgell. Day 116 included a climb to the famous Spanish mountain crags of Monistrol de Montserrat, an elevation of 690 metres. Day 117 to Barcelona covered a distance of 97 kilometres and marked the end of stage 5—from Athens, a distance of 3,787 kilometres.

Following a two-day layover in the beautiful city of Barcelona, all 240 riders and staff of Odyssey 2000 were transported by coach for the fourteen-hour (overnight) journey to Gibraltar, which was the start of stage 6 to Lisbon. We arrived at Gibraltar at around 10 a.m. on day 120, feeling rather tired and jaded after our night journey from Barcelona. There was one rest day in Gibraltar before stage 6, which would end in Lisbon on May 1.

This had to be one of the shortest stages for the whole year. The next few days' route was familiar to me, and no doubt many UK tourists. It took us through the popular tourist towns of Torremolinos, Motril, Granada, and Cordoba.

In Seville, we had another rest day, where the Odyssey riders went their different ways to relax and explore. For some (but not yours truly), it included a bullfight in Seville.

In our travels over the past four months, it had become evident how popular and well established the Irish brewing industry is around the world. I refer, of course, to the traditional Irish pub, where the best Guinness can be found outside Ireland. No one can locate a good (Irish) watering hole like a thirsty cyclist, such as when Odyssey 2000 rode into Seville. A particularly international flavour surrounded the Irish pub we found in Seville. There, a mixture of American, Canadian, French, and Swiss cyclists and one New Zealand cyclist were served by an English-speaking French waiter.

After we left Seville, our route took us into Portugal for a brief three days' cycling to Lisbon, which ended stage 6.

41

Stage 7

**USA and Canada
(Washington, DC, to
Quebec)**

1,811 kilometres

12 May to 6 June 2000

On day 133, May 12, the Odyssey cavalcade flew from Lisbon to Washington, DC, for a five-day layover period. This was a welcome break for all concerned, in particular those in the party who were within travelling time from home.

Having spent ten days in the area back in 1995 following my coast-to-coast ride, I was very grateful for some hospitality from my dear friends Bob and Cindy Roser, who live just forty miles south of Washington, DC. This layover gave me a chance to catch up with friends in the area, write general correspondence, write in my journal, and do a little shopping.

On May 18, we departed from Washington, DC, for the rather tough five days' ride to New York City, where we had another two rest days. The rest period in New York was not long enough, with so much to see and do.

It was on day 143 that Odyssey 2000 rode into New York City. Had we arrived together, and ridden in formation with a police escort, it would have been an impressive sight, similar to the Rose Parade. As it happened, the forty-mile ride from our campsite at Cheesequake, New Jersey, with the subsequent congestion and bridges, did much to split the 240-odd cyclists. From our point of view, we still had a very impressive entry into this great city. It was by the five-mile ferry ride from Staten Island past the Statue of Liberty that we entered New York City.

We had a ride through the city to our hostel, which was situated in Central Park North and on the edge of Harlem. We were told that this area had not been safe to walk in alone five years ago. Thanks to the NYPD and the new zero-tolerance regime now in operation, I am pleased to report that we safely walked and cycled through Central Park, plus the downtown area.

We departed from New York City before 8 a.m. on 25 May, at the height of morning rush hour. No experienced cyclist, unless he or she were local, would consider this a wise move. However, thanks to our well-planned route sheet, we took to the backstreets and over the George Washington Bridge via numerous cycle tracks. By late afternoon, we were 101 miles north of New York City at the Kittatinny Campground in a remote part of New York State.

Five days and 512 miles later, we arrived in the capital of Canada. I refer, of course, to the beautiful city of Ottawa. Here, we were treated to some luxury on the accommodation side, housed in the residence halls at Carleton University.

Ottawa

The presence of 240 cycles and riders is not easy to conceal in any location, particularly when the media have done their bit. So the professional bike thieves in Ottawa helped themselves to three Odyssey cycles, which had all been securely locked up in the city centre on our layover day. What made this incident even more frustrating for one couple, who were victims, was that they had just spent the equivalent of six hundred pounds each to upgrade their cycles and replace all worn accessories. Plus, due to the nature of this trip, the Odyssey cycles were not insurable.

The remainder of stage 7 took us east along the St Lawrence River to Montreal and Quebec. Including rest days, this covered a period of six days. During this time, the weather was kind, and we were again housed at two of Canada's top universities at Montreal and Quebec. Both cities were new to me, and we were reminded here of the French connection, particularly in Quebec, a beautiful city which is more French than many major French cities. On 5 June, we had our final layover day in North America, and yours truly celebrated his birthday, sixty-eight years young. That reminded me of a quote I had recently heard, which said, "Growing old is compulsory, *but* growing up is optional."

The following day, we flew to Paris for the start of stage 8 to Aberdeen.

Odyssey 2000 arrived in Paris from Quebec early on 7 June. Because stage 8 would be on home territory for me, I had promised myself some time off during this stage so I could catch up with my family and a few other personal matters, which do accumulate when you are away for such an extended period. My proposed period off the tour would cover the twelve-day period from Paris to London, which meant that I had to officially sign off. Early evening that same day, I was reunited with one-third of my family when I flew into Southampton.

However, a complete rest from the bike for that period was not to be, as three of my American Odyssey companions were anxious to complete a UK audax randonneur ride. So against my better judgement, I was persuaded to join them; it was, after all, only a two-hundred-kilometre ride with a start and finish in Salisbury and not too far from one of my family. That took place on 18 June, and two days later, we rejoined the Odyssey party in London.

The UK route then took us to Winchester, with the midday checkpoint at Cyclists Touring Club HQ at Godalming in Surrey. I am reminded here of an amusing incident that occurred whilst I was riding through the leafy suburbs of Surrey with a group of around twenty-four companions. I was (as usual) bringing up the rear as the group approached a junction with a pedestrian crossing, and no pedestrian in sight. However, before half the group had passed over the crossing, a very smart senior gent appeared at the crossing and waited impatiently. In awe as we sped by, he looked from one cyclist to another as if we were aliens from outer space. Shaking his head as I passed by, the senior gent looked at me and said, "And you b***** are old enough to know better."

The next stage took us from Winchester to Bath, where we were due for another rest day, and this took me into my own territory. There, all my companions looked to me for advice on points of interest. Also, it had been planned from the start of Odyssey that those interested would have the option of an organised ride and a pub lunch on the layover day in Bath.

Thanks to the efforts of Dave Amesbury and the Bristol Cyclists Touring Club, the ride was a great success, with over eighty turning out. On a layover day, this was unheard of. I am not quite sure whether the unofficial ride or the pub lunch at Bradford-on-Avon was the main attraction.

Odyssey 2000 in Bath with the Bristol CTC

Odyssey 2000's arrival in England and Wales coincided with the Millennium Festival of Cycling. Jointly organised by Cyclists Touring Club and Sustrans, this festival celebrated the opening of five thousand miles of the National Cycle Network. Having looked in advance at the proposed Odyssey route through England and Wales, I decided to go off route and use as much of the network as possible over the next few days. This plan was circulated to my Odyssey companions, and much to my surprise, something like eighty of them decided to join me. From Bath to Cardiff, my group and I took a route along the Bath to Bristol cycleway and over the old Severn Bridge into Wales.

When I first registered for Odyssey back in 1996, I had no idea that there would be an overnight stop in Cardiff and just fifteen miles from my home in the Vale of Glamorgan. From Cardiff, the itinerary said we would go north to Holyhead en route to Ireland. However, I planned to continue to use the National Cycle Network along the Lon Las Cymru, known in South Wales as the Taff Trail. Again, at least eighty of my companions fully supported this, and luckily for all of us, but me in particular, the weather all the way from Bath to North Wales was excellent. We had overnight stops at Builth Wells and Barmouth. This must have been the only period in the whole year that I did not need to refer to the official route sheet.

During the last few days in Wales, I began to think to myself, *I can do Ireland and Scotland anytime (like when I get older)*. So when Odyssey left Barmouth for Holyhead and Ireland, yours truly signed off and took the train back to Bristol to complete my three Rs: reading, writing, and relaxation. Then on 8 July, I took the train, with bike and baggage, to the Granite City of Aberdeen, where I would rendezvous with Odyssey on 11 July prior to the start of the next stage commencing in Scandinavia.

Not many folk who venture into a world cycle tour have the chance to visit family and friends halfway around the world, but this was my good fortune in recent weeks. And I had the opportunity as we approached the point of no return; in other words, before we passed into the second half of our bike ride around the world, I had the chance to reflect on the previous six months and anticipate what may be in store for the rest of the year.

At this stage of Odyssey, I thought that it was indeed the experience of a lifetime, albeit a very demanding one. I did have a few dark moments when I thought, *What the heck am I doing here? There must be easier ways to see the world.* Having said that, you couldn't possibly cover this itinerary within one year if you undertook a solo or self-organised trip. When you have a preplanned itinerary, two meals a day, and a bed or campsite organised for you, it makes the daily ritual of getting on your bike and riding for six to nine hours more manageable and acceptable.

Odyssey 2000 also made me appreciate the many things we take for granted at home, and how much we have near our own doorstep in the UK and Europe. Europe has so much natural beauty, combined with the culture and history, compared with the New World. I, too, appreciated the fact that we were burning many calories every day, which gave us an opportunity to indulge in gastronomic delicacies in many countries on our itinerary, without putting on weight.

This all brings me to stage 9.

Following our one-hour flight from the Granite City of Aberdeen to Bergen, Norway, we were greeted by typical English weather. It was cold, wet, and windy, not a very bright outlook for the start of stage 9. My first impression of Norway was it is a land with abundant mountains and fjords, a creation of natural beauty. It is a land where the road traveller has to contend with many bridges, tunnels, and ferries.

Hills of Norway

It is also a land where a pint of beer will set you back almost four pounds. So in the interest of economy, yours truly found it advisable to review the customary pre-dinner habit.

47

We departed Bergen on day 195 with the weather much improved for the hundred-kilometre ride to Risnes. Within three hours, we were either climbing over the mountains or riding through them via a tunnel.

On our third day in Norway, I overheard (in the shower) an amusing conversation between two of my Odyssey companions. It appeared that one of them had become involved in conversation with a local Norwegian. The local had enquired about our itinerary, such as where we had come from and where we were going. "We are heading for Oslo," said my friend.

But the local said, "You are going the wrong way!"

"Yes," said my friend, "you may be right, but we go via the scenic route, which is usually over the mountain, and if I need supper and a bed tonight, then I have to go this way."

We arrived in Oslo after a very hard six days, riding over 717 kilometres and numerous mountain passes from 2,500 to 4,000 feet in elevation. So we were ready for a rest day. As usual, with our Odyssey layover days, one day was not enough to cover all that we would have liked to do and see.

What this stage in particular made me appreciate was how much I had forgotten from my school history lessons. I therefore intend to include in my reflections some of the main points of interest.

Oslo has a current population of 500,000, and over 10 per cent of the country's total population has a very turbulent history. Oslo was founded long after the Vikings had developed the town. In 1348, the Black Death wiped out almost half the population. Then in 1624, the city was completely destroyed by fire.

In more recent times, Oslo has become the focal point for the Nobel Foundation's annual awards. These were set up by the Swedish inventor and industrialist Alfred Nobel.

We departed from Oslo on day 202, 19 July. There is much more I could say about this city, which is set in beautiful surroundings. 2000 was the anniversary of its own foundation one thousand years before.

After twenty-five years of political debate, the Norwegian electorate decided in 1994 that it did not wish to be part of the European community. Whilst Norway has one of the highest costs of living in Europe, its standard of living and welfare benefits equal the best.

Two days after leaving Oslo, we crossed into Sweden, with overnight stops at Lysekil and Gothenburg, which is the hub of a great walking centre. From Gothenburg, we would take the three-hour ferry ride to Frederikshavn in Denmark.

I noticed a marked difference in the terrain in Denmark, which is low-lying with many small islands. The whole of Scandinavia also showed a marked improvement in infrastructure (compared with other countries). It has many good cycle tracks, which were a great asset to us when entering or leaving a built-up area.

On day 207 (25 July), we arrived in Copenhagen, Denmark's capital, with the prospect of having 26 July off. Whilst a day off the bike was always welcome, I had found that the amount of walking we did on those days while sightseeing could be just as tiring as biking, and Copenhagen was no exception.

Mermaid in Copenhagen

I'm not quite sure whether it was the Odyssey company I was keeping, but whenever we arrived at a location that brewed alcohol, an educational (?) visit seemed to appear on our agenda. In March, we had the pleasure of visiting some of South Africa's famous vineyards. Now in Copenhagen, it was the world-famous Carlsberg Brewery which got the stamp of our approval over two free glasses of the famous brew. The Carlsberg Brewery was founded in 1873, but it was not until 1903 that Carlsberg and its competitor Tuborg signed an agreement to share all profits and losses. The two companies merged in 1970.

Today, 88 per cent of Carlsberg Group beer sales are generated outside of Denmark. The beer is brewed in seventy-two production sites in forty countries. The group's most important markets in Europe are headed by, *yes*, the UK. The company now boasts that every single day of the year, over thirty million people around the world enjoy a Carlsberg product (end of commercial).

The next major destination on our itinerary was beautiful Stockholm, capital city of Sweden. This required four days of riding, a total of 650 kilometres. I think that stage 9 in Scandinavia gets a very high mark in my Odyssey book for all-round satisfaction. A majority agreed that we had first-class food and accommodation. It was also a plus to find that the local population in each country we visited spoke English so widely.

Whilst each of the Scandinavian capital cities offered something special, I feel that Stockholm would go to the top of my list for beauty, location, and variety of interests and activities. The city is composed of fourteen islands, creating a wealth of waterways for the very large sailing community. To the north and south of Stockholm, there are around twenty-four thousand islands, many of which are uninhabited.

On 1 August, we started the eighth month of Odyssey 2000 by catching the 8.30 a.m. ferry from Stockholm to Turku, Finland. The Odyssey cavalcade had moved from one country to another by numerous means of transportation since January 1. However, our journey from Stockholm to Turku by the eleven-hour luxury ferry was one of the most relaxing journeys we had undertaken.

The weather was good, and the route wound its way among the archipelago of islands from Sweden to Finland. The ferry unloaded its cargo and passengers at Turku around 7 p.m. We then had a sixteen-kilometre ride to the hostel where we were due to spend the night. The hostels and campsite facilities in Finland were some of the best in Scandinavia. The terrain was much easier, and the weather was good for our two days of riding to Helsinki.

Finland is composed of 70 per cent forest and 10 per cent water; the winters are long and severe, and summers are short and warm. From my brief interlude here and later in Russia, I found it difficult to appreciate that, prior to 1917, Finland was part of Russia because the difference in the quality of life today between the two countries is so marked.

The original Odyssey itinerary promised a few days' cycling in Russia. However, due to logistical or diplomatic problems, we could not take our support vehicles into the country. A compromise was therefore put forward for our consideration. Our five-day layover in Helsinki would include an optional two- or three-day train excursion to St Petersburg. The tour organisers had already accounted for the cost of our accommodation; yours truly (along with eighty other Odyssey folk) went for the two-day option.

In view of the visa requirements for entry into Russia, we had needed to submit our applications via a Finnish travel agent three weeks before the visit. Once again, I noted how British and American passport holders were treated differently around the world. Whilst our American companions were obliged to pay forty-five dollars for the visa, I and the other UK member, John, were issued a visa free of charge.

There are two trains which make the six-hour daily journey from Helsinki to St Petersburg. The first departs at 6.30 a.m., the second at 2 p.m. It was pure luck that we decided to take the early train, which is Finnish; the second is Russian. Our companions who chose to take the late train made many critical comments. We later confirmed them when we experienced the standard and quality of public transportation in Russia.

As the train approached the Russian border, we were informed that the restaurant car would be closed and all toilets would be locked. Shortly after this, all passports were collected, and the Russian customs and immigration staff came on board to inspect *all* passports. It was discreetly commented on that the Russian authorities may call into question such a large contingent of visitors from the USA. But then they confirmed we were a harmless bunch of bikers.

My first impression of Russia in general and St Petersburg in particular was that the country was sadly in need of all the everyday things we take for granted. It had much poverty in all walks of life. I saw no evidence of any recent development; in fact, most public and private buildings were in a dilapidated state. Seeing it felt like turning the clock back fifty-odd years; buses and trains alike appeared to need much attention. Having said that, St Petersburg is still regarded as one of the world's largest and most beautiful cities. It has some of the most exquisite, unmatched buildings in the world.

Church of the Resurrection (St Petersburg)

The city was, after all, the capital of the Russian Empire for over two centuries; that status ended after the Bolshevik Revolution in 1918. Construction of the city began at the height of the Great Northern War, when a fortress was needed to defend the gate to the Baltic, which the Russians had won. Peter the Great founded the city in 1703, so any cultural historians (which I am not) would be in their element here.

My two-day excursion was an experience which I will not forget. With so much to see and limited time at our disposal, our many guided tour bookings did record business. The three-hour city tour which we selected was led by a very good English-speaking guide who later turned out to be a professor of mathematics trying to make ends meet. Whilst I can only marvel at the beauty of the Winter and Summer Palaces and the Church of the Resurrection, and the wealth within the Hermitage, one must feel for the man in the street who has suffered at the hands of one system after another, and is still struggling in spite of the wealth around him.

Fortunately, we returned to Helsinki by the Finnish train, which got us back to the city with thirty-six hours to spare before our flight to start stage 10 in Berlin. So ended stage 9, a cycling distance of 2,271 kilometres, plus many more by ferry. Look out for stage 10 from Berlin to Amsterdam.

A two-hour flight took us from Helsinki to Berlin on day 222 (9 August). We arrived in the evening, and what a contrast to St Petersburg we saw.

Today's Berlin has to do with what happened in November 1989—the Wall fell. Berlin had been divided for twenty-eight years. The efforts to restore the city have made it just about the biggest construction site in Europe, and the largest to be undertaken in modern history.

In view of the limited time at our disposal, a large number of Odyssey riders elected to undertake a city tour conducted by cycle! In four hours, we covered the Victory Column, Brandenburg Gate, Potsdamer Platz, Checkpoint Charlie, the site of Hitler's bunker, the Reichstag, Bebelplatz (the site of Nazi book burning), and the remains of the 155-kilometre Wall.

Berliner Dom Mit Fernsehturm (Berlin)

Our departure from Berlin went smoothly, but not our approach to the city of Dresden. A combination of cobblestones and tramlines had the disastrous effect of bringing down five Odyssey riders, one of whom needed hospital treatment. It is difficult for today's visitor to Dresden to appreciate that Allied bombing destroyed 85 per cent of the city in 1945. Rebuilding the city to its former glory has been the top priority of the city's fathers over the years. Many buildings now stand in their former glory, but there is still much to be done.

The city's harmony with the River Elbe is impressive. That and the fact that parks and gardens take up 60 per cent of the city area make it a place to want to linger. However, it was not possible for me to linger as I would have liked to, as on day 225, we were heading for the Czech Republic.

The Czech Republic is at the heart of Europe and made for pleasant cycling, with its rolling countryside, wooded hills, and fertile valleys. Whilst the quality of life in general still lags behind that of its neighbours, it has made great strides since the former Czechoslovakia freed itself from Soviet satellite status in 1990.

We arrived in the beautiful city of Prague, where we were to spend two nights. Our campsite was on the outskirts of the city, which gave us the opportunity to use the public transport system, which is reputed to be one of the best in Europe. We departed from Prague on day 228 for the three days' ride to Salzburg, Austria, via Passau, with its dramatic change in scenery. This also meant that we were back in the hills.

From Salzburg, we headed for Munich, with an increase in daily temperatures. This changed briefly as we entered Munich following a long and hot day. Approximately three kilometres from our destination, we were greeted by a violent thunderstorm.

The Odyssey 2000 experience helps you understand and wonder at the lifestyles of citizens around the world. Germany, for example, has its many biergartens, very popular places to socialize. The Germans appear to be the world's greatest lovers of garden gnomes and sausages. There are a reputed thirty-five million garden gnomes around the country. And for the gourmet sausage lover, there are 1,456 different varieties of sausages. The Germans also have chip distributors and a home delivery service for condoms—not quite sure what, if any, connection there is there.

The route from Munich took us to Oberammergau, famous for its passion play held every ten years. And guess what? Odyssey picked the year and time for the play. It would have been very difficult for an Odyssey rider to attend the passion play, as I understand it lasts around nine hours and has an audience of five thousand.

The itinerary then took us into Switzerland via Braz and very briefly through another country, Liechtenstein, making it one of the shortest cross-country rides. On it, we covered a distance of around twenty-five kilometres. This is where we started climbing again, with a four-thousand-foot climb over the last fourteen kilometres into the mountain resort of Flims. Here, we had a rest day before tackling the route to Raron via Andermatt. We then rode into some of the most spectacular scenery we had seen to date.

Switzerland

On 25 August, we had a very pleasant eighty-six-kilometre ride from Chatel to Geneva, and following a long descent, we rode along the banks of Lake Geneva. Around twenty-eight kilometres from Geneva, we stopped for lunch at the historic and medieval village of Yvoire. Here, we locked up our bikes and meander around the cobbled streets of this beautiful lakeside village.

Just ten kilometres from lunch, we were invited to indulge in a glass of wine, plus cheese and biscuits, arranged by one Gilbert Filchard, who was the only Odyssey rider from France. Gilbert, a retired pharmacist from Lyon, spent the first twenty years of his life here. He is part shareholder in a family vineyard along with his brother and ninety-year-old mother, who has a reputation for driving fast cars.

Geneva is a beautiful city which has it all and appears to cater to the well-heeled Porsche owner, as well as the modest cyclist. I was not aware of this, but Geneva is known as the City of Refuges. It has earned this reputation by making its extensive bomb shelters available to those in need from around the world, the latest being the Bosnian refugees. Now, it was the turn of two-hundred-odd homeless and itinerant bikers on their way around the world to use this accommodation. We had stayed in an assortment of hotels and hostels since January, but I must admit this was just about the most unusual accommodation to date.

Constructed at the height of the Cold War, the bunkers took us the equivalent of three stories below ground. One entered each level via a large doorway with an eighteen-inch-thick door constructed of steel and concrete; walls were two metres thick. My first reaction to this was claustrophobia. But my fear was unfounded; in spite of the fact that there were around forty-eight bunks per dormitory, they were spacious, with air conditioning throughout. Adequate toilet facilities and showers, together with medical sections, would enable a large number to live in reasonable comfort for some time. Fortunately, our experience was limited to two nights only.

Two days later, we arrived at the spa town of Bad Zurzach, which I found to be a friendly little town with an illustrious history. As we arrived at the campsite on the outskirts of the town, the residents lining the street gave us an ovation. On the banks of the River Rhine, the site was primarily a residential and vacation caravan park.

Bad Zurzach became famous when, on 5 September 1955, drilling successfully discovered a warm spring at 1,400 feet below ground. Since that date, six hundred litres of healing water have gushed from the ground every minute. So all year round now, visitors can take advantage of the thermal baths' unique bathing pleasures. Doctors recommend the Bad Zurzach thermal spring for anyone suffering from rheumatic diseases of the spine, joints, and cartilage, as well as for anyone needing follow-up for injuries and accidents.

It was lucky that this, our last stop in Switzerland, was a rest day. Suffice to say that many Odyssey bikers (including yours truly) relaxed in the spacious spa complex with its numerous pools and whirlpools. So it was a relaxed and refreshed bunch of Odyssey riders who set out on day 243.

Two days later, we were back in Germany, at Koblenz. With only one night here, we were not able to fully appreciate what the locals call this *beautiful corner of Germany*; the town sits at the junction of the Rhine and the Moselle. Needless to say that for the next two days, we rode along the River Moselle with vineyards as far as we could see. A good bike trail along the river should have made for a pleasant ride, but with a change in the weather, we had almost two days of continuous rain.

John. On 1st September I was riding beside the River Rhine.where i encountered Elbert our oldest rider.. Elbert was that day celebrating his 80th birthday. It was cold and wet and at the time we were slightly lost He said he had come on Odyssey so he could think what to do with the rest of his life! Should I survive to be 80 I too would like to be out on my bike, but only if it's not raining, and preferably if I'm not lost.

We arrived in Luxembourg on 3 September, with just four days' riding to Amsterdam, where we would have a five-day break before our flight to Australia. Having covered the 4,540 kilometres and two stages from Norway, yours truly was ready for a break. Total cycling distance since January 1: 22,415 kilometres. Only five folks had ridden every kilometre so far.

My next report will be from down under.

Greetings, folks (from down under, where spring has just arrived). At 6.40 a.m. on Sunday, 17 September, Canberra was invaded by 220 yellow-helmeted cyclists, looking rather bleary-eyed and ready for a bed.

It pleases me to say that after a smooth but twenty-two-hour flight from Cologne, our DC-10 charter flight took the Odyssey cavalcade down under for the start of stage 11. There was a welcome refuelling stop ten hours into the flight at Sri Lanka, which made the travelling time from Cologne to Canberra nearly thirty hours.

Unfortunately, Canberra Airport is only geared up for domestic flights. This means it normally has no customs or immigration staff on hand, and the authorities here are rather fussy about who and what is allowed into the country. Arising from this, customs and immigration staff were brought in to process the 250-odd passengers on the DC-10, who were allowed off the plane forty at a time. This included being approved by sniffer dogs trained in looking for drugs. Regrettably, one male Odyssey rider was found to be carrying an undesirable substance and was asked to leave the tour and country forthwith.

John. Before we left the police gave us a lecture on how to ride a bicycle safely. We were a bit taken aback as after 8 months riding we thought we knew all about safe riding. The lecture ended with the warning to watch out for 'drop bears'. This turns out to be an Australian joke on the basis of a large carnivorous version of the koala which drops on it's prey from a great height. II don't think any of us lost any sleep worrying about these mythical beasts

Having spent six months in Australia four years prior, I came partly prepared for a welcome return. Unfortunately, many of my travelling companions did not come so prepared. This was confirmed by a headline in the *Canberra Times* on 18 September: "World Cyclists Shocked by Dead Roos" (kangaroos). I am not quite sure of the ratio of kangaroos to cars in Australia; I think the latter could be increasing, with some doubts about the former.

Whilst Australia has plenty of space for both kangaroos and cars, it is a sad fact of life that the nocturnal habits of the kangaroos has affected their health and population. The first two days here, I personally saw six dead kangaroos along the side of the road. The problem for kangaroos and car drivers alike is that the kangaroos only come out after nightfall; they have no road sense (and do not wear helmets). It has a fatal effect on the kangaroos in most cases. I assume it can badly damage the car, and in some cases, the driver does not survive the impact.

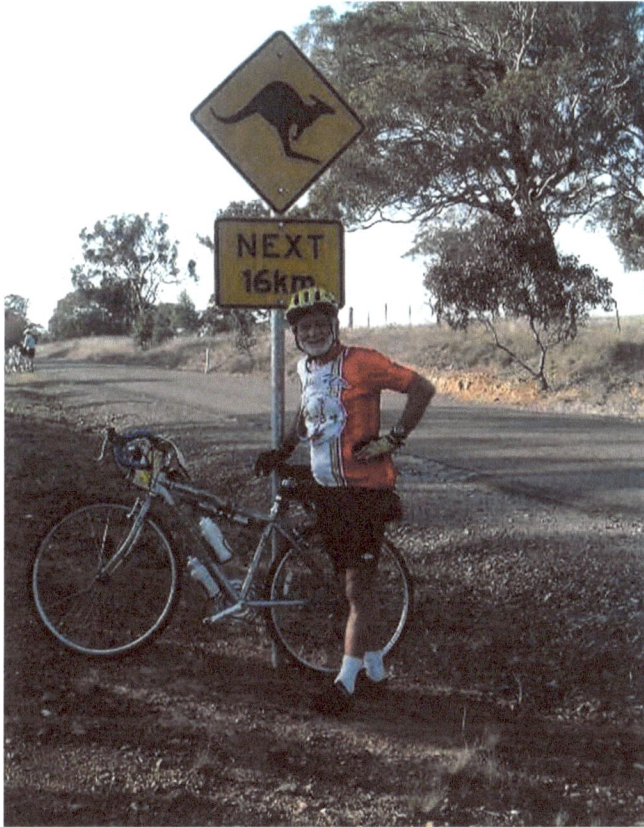

From the Twenty-Seventh Olympiad in Sydney, on Saturday, 23 September, two English cyclists had an introduction to baseball. This was the first, and possibly only, opportunity which John and I would have to watch nine grown men take turns throwing a small cowhide ball ninety miles per hour at one of their opposing team.

In baseball, the lone opposing player has only a thirty-two-inch-long wooden bat with which to defend himself. Provided the ball is thrown correctly, the player with the bat has only three attempts to strike the ball. If he fails to strike the ball, he is then relieved of his post and must return to his teammates hiding in the changing room. That is our brief description of an American-style ball game; I hope it will not offend too many of my friends across the pond. They do, after all, pull our leg over the complexity of cricket.

America had been winning its fair share of gold medals, but right then, the US baseball team was trailing Cuba 6 to 1. We were told that this was not the cream of US ballplayers, and they had gotten together only a month before.

Yours truly was planning to relax on the coast of New South Wales, where Odyssey 2000 had a four-day layover. I did not have tickets for the Olympic Games and had no plans to visit Sydney. So when three Odyssey companions who had spare tickets invited me to join them, my initial reaction was to decline the invite. Then I thought, *How many sixty-eight-year-old pensioners at home would decline an offer like this?* and *Am I likely to be around for the next games?* So I decided to accept the offer of tickets. On 23 September, we had tickets for the morning field and track events and the baseball in the evening, and on Sunday, there were tickets for tennis.

Having now attended all three events, I am pleased that I went to my first Olympic Games. I was particularly impressed with the friendly and efficient organisation behind the games. Moving thousands of spectators to and from Olympic Park on the outskirts of Sydney was no mean feat. Anyone considering using a car was told to forget it. Included in the cost of our tickets was free transport on all buses and trains in the Sydney suburban rail network. Double-decker trains ran to and from Olympic Park every three to four minutes, with each train taking over three thousand passengers at a time. This service was operating from numerous city and suburban stations.

The Sydney press proudly conveyed the statistic that the specially constructed Olympic stadium was the largest purpose-built outdoor venue in Olympic history, seating 110,000 people. The stadium's main arch was 295 metres long, the length of three rugby fields (try line to try line). So when the stadium was to capacity (mainly with full-voiced Aussies), I found it a moving experience.

Yes, I am still in Oz (just), and with only three days left before we take off for Japan, this may be my last report from Oz. We are about to leave the familiarity of the Western world. Having entirely devoted the last update to my visit to the Olympic Games, I now resume with my reflections on Odyssey 2000 and its brief visit en route to the Sydney area.

My previous visit to Canberra four years prior had lasted for six weeks, so there was no need for any sightseeing on my part. When we had a welcome rest day after our long flight from Germany, I was very grateful for the hospitality which I had from David Fraser as well as Bruce and Coral King, a much-travelled and lovable couple. We then had two hard days' riding, over 290 kilometres from Canberra to Wollongong on the coast of New South Wales south of Sydney. This was to be one of our longer layover periods. We were housed at the East Campus of Wollongong University, which was a ninety-minute train ride from Sydney and a good choice.

The final leg of our Aussie tour was a five-day ride from Townsville on the coast of Queensland to Cairns. This required a two-hour flight from Sydney. On arrival in Townsville, we were reunited with our bikes and luggage, which had travelled three days by road from Wollongong.

The next English-speaking region we would travel to was New Zealand, which we would reach in December. And it would be thirteen weeks before this epic bike ride came to a final halt in California. Taking this into account, plus the fact that I was looking to do a little leisurely exploration of North Queensland on my own, yours truly decided to go off route for the five days between Townsville and Cairns.

An attraction for me was the Great Barrier Reef, which was accessible from either Cairns or Townsville. As the latter boasts 230 days of sunshine per year, versus the periodic tropical rainstorms in the Cairns region, I decided to stay put in Townsville, which also had another attraction.

On 6 June 1770, when Captain Cook was sailing up the east coast of Australia, he spotted a small island just eight kilometres off the coast, which he called *Magnetic Island*. On 28 September 2000, the island was rediscovered by one globe-trotting pensioner from Wales. During the intervening period, many others from around the world have rediscovered it. Still known as Magnetic Island, it has a unique blend of national parks and some of the best beaches and most picturesque bays in Queensland. During my two-day visit, I was informed that in 1968, the population of Magnetic Island was 290; this has now increased to over 2,000 (excluding visiting tourists).

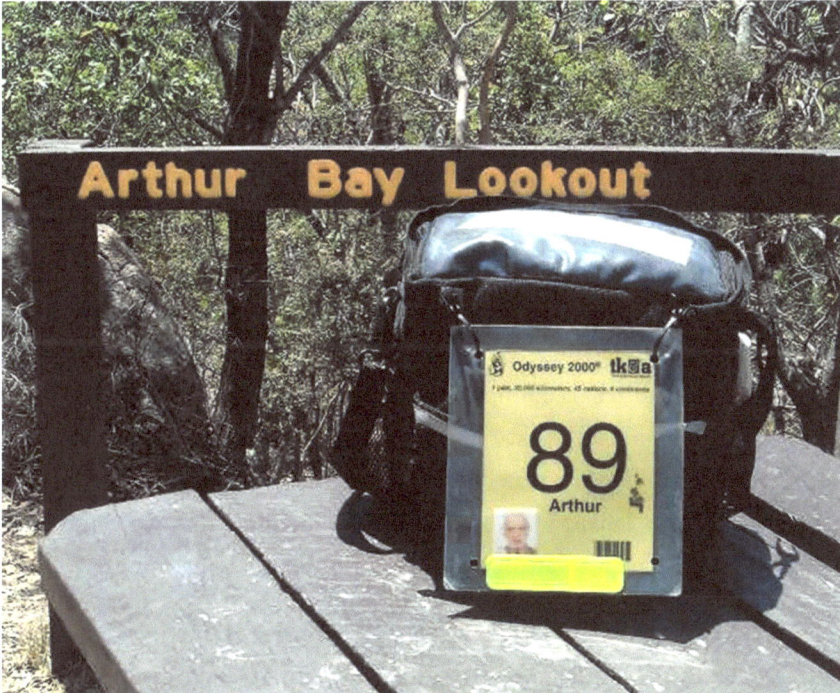

Having spent two days on the island and one day on the reef, where I indulged in my first taste of snorkelling, I then took the five-hour coach journey to Cairns, where I reunited with the Odyssey party. My first night in Cairns, I decided to eat at a smart restaurant by the name of Dundee's. One item on the menu caught my eye: "The Real Aussie Adventure: Tender slices of buffalo, emu sausage, barramundi with skewered kangaroo and crocodile. Served with a selection of Dundee's special sauces." (I had grilled trout.)

Look out for the next update from Japan, at the start of stage 12 in Asia.

Greetings from Japan. I left Cairns on 4 October, one day behind schedule and in style, en route to Japan via Malaysia. I had not had the pleasure (or the resources) to fly first class before, but on our flight to Malaysia, yours truly was given the VIP treatment of the first-class upper section of a Boeing 747. This area was normally reserved for Odyssey staff, but on this flight, the extra space was allocated to the select few who had ridden every mile since January. In addition, space was allocated for the group's most senior members, which was when I discovered that there were only four folk older than me. *Is that possible?* I thought.

After two flights, we arrived in Japan *without our cycles*. This section of Odyssey 2000 was fraught with complications. The transfer of 240 bodies and bikes, plus luggage, had run into problems before we left Australia. It was not clear whether the complications were logistical, diplomatic, or political. I suspect one of the latter.

We had received changes to the Odyssey itinerary at a meeting in Cairns on 2 October. We were advised that the Malaysian Boeing 747, a charter plane, that we would be using from now till December had been unable to obtain landing clearance in Japan. Arising from this, our Malaysian Boeing 747 took the bikes and us to Kuala Lumpur, where we were split into two scheduled Japan Airlines flights to Osaka. Two days after that, we were informed that the bikes were still in Malaysia. There was also the possibility that if the bikes were brought into Japan, we would have no guarantee that we could take them out on the date we were due to leave for Hong Kong en route to China.

Having had a few days off the bike in Australia, I was looking forward to getting back in the saddle, although I did not relish the prospect of cycling 130-odd kilometres on a bowl of rice and noodles. This was not to be, however, as our Japan itinerary had now become a coach tour. A coach tour with 230 cyclists was something none of us had anticipated. As someone said, it was all part of the adventure, albeit a very expensive one. (As we found out, its cost of living is one of the highest, after Norway's.)

After nine months and over forty countries, the initial reaction of all concerned upon reaching Japan was that we were about to undergo a major culture shock—not just in Japan but also all over in the next five weeks.

For the benefit of those not familiar with this area, Japan consists of four major islands, which stretch less than one thousand miles. About 80 per cent of the population of 124 million people (just under half the USA's population) resides on the central island of Honshu, which is where our itinerary took us.

Japan has over three thousand smaller, mainly volcanic islands and over sixty active volcanoes. Historically, major earthquakes have occurred around every sixty years (with one overdue).

Following our arrival in Japan at Osaka's Kansai International Airport, we were faced with a two-hour-plus coach journey to our hotel in Kyoto. This was one stretch of road which very few cyclists would wish to venture on. The bulk of this journey covered a densely populated and industrialised area.

We were booked into our hotel for two nights, giving us a free day to explore Kyoto, which has the reputation of being Japan's major cultural centre. The first impression of Kyoto, as with other major cities in Japan, is the glare of neon by night and large-scale urban ugliness. However, this city's beauty is there if you have the time to seek it out. As usual, our time was limited, so we had a four-hour English guided walk, which covered one of the largest Buddhist temples in Japan. While Kyoto has its eyes on the future, its past is very much in evidence. It was the imperial capital from 794 to 1868. It has more than two thousand temples and shrines, three palaces, and dozens of gardens and museums.

As always, I couldn't help but notice certain aspects of life in a new country. In this case, I noticed that drivers of one fleet of taxis were very smartly dressed with white gloves and bow ties. I also noticed that hotel bedroom doors in Japan are considerably smaller than those in Western hotels. Then there were the restaurants, which display their menu and prices in the window in the form of a plastic meal. In our case, we took the waiter to the window to indicate our choice.

The itinerary from Kyoto took us to the coastal town of Amanohashidate on the north-west of the island. This, we were told, was a popular tourist attraction; with another rest day ahead and with no bikes, it was time for some serious walking.

At the end of a long and hilly walk, I had the great pleasure of being introduced to a Japanese bathhouse. We were advised the facility was part of a large hotel complex. There, four of us presented ourselves at reception. This will be my last update from Japan, so I will now extol the virtues and gory details of a Japanese bathhouse.

Having paid our entry fee of eight hundred yen (approximately five pounds), we were ushered to the bathhouse entrance at the rear of the hotel. At this point, we were required to remove our footwear and were given a pair of sandals. We then passed into the male changing rooms, where *all* our clothes were placed into a basket and exchanged for one small and two large towels.

At this point, I began to feel rather vulnerable, but as I was not alone, I thought, *When in Rome (or Japan)*. We then went into a large room with marble tile floors and walls. Around three sides of this room were shower fittings one metre above floor level, with a mirror above. And below was a low plastic stool together with two containers of body soap and shampoo. In the absence of other bathers, we would have been dubious as to the next procedure. Luckily for us, numerous honourable gentlemen of all ages sat at the stools in various stages of soaping and showering their bodies. Some were shaving, hence the mirror.

Having cleansed our bodies, we then entered a long, narrow hot bath filled to a depth of around four feet. At the end of this bath was a glass sliding door. Following a relaxing fifteen-minute soak, our curiosity got the better of us, and we ventured through the sliding door. At this point, I did rather feel that one bath indoors was OK, but to go outside for another did seem to be overdoing it. Having said that, I found the surroundings very relaxing. Bench seats were scattered around an open courtyard, with senior Japanese businessmen deep in conversation with nothing but a very small towel to cover their modesty. The hot bath to one side of the courtyard was oval shaped with fountains and rocks. There were a sloping garden and trees beyond, all of which in floodlight. At the end of our second soak in the open, we all agreed that this was indeed a very civilized and sociable way to spend an hour or two.

We had two more days left of our coach tour in Japan, with the penultimate night's stop at an idyllic island by the name of Miyajima. This island is a very short ferry ride from Hiroshima, where we spent three hours to visit the Hiroshima Peace Memorial Park, which I found to be a very moving experience.

Anyone who was under ten years of age on 6 August 1945 (I was thirteen) can be forgiven for not knowing that at 8.15 a.m. on this date, Hiroshima fell victim to the world's first atomic bomb. Arising from this tragic event, only one building in the centre of the city predates 1945. The building, known as the Atomic Bomb Dome, is just across the river from Peace Memorial Park. Before the bomb exploded directly above it in 1945, it was known as Industrial Promotion Hall.

The intense heat rays and blast caused by the bomb crushed and burned every building within two kilometres of the epicentre. By the end of 1945, when the effects of radiation had subsided, it was confirmed that up to 140,000 lives had been lost. The propped-up ruins of the Atomic Bomb Dome have been left as an eternal reminder of the tragedy. It is to be hoped that future generations will remember this tragedy so they prevent it from ever happening again.

On this sombre note, I take my leave of you at midday on 12 October as we leave Japan en route to China.

Greetings from China

What a contrast exists between China and Japan. But both countries face major social and economic problems which one cannot fail to notice.

Japan has an ageing population and a falling birth rate. The high cost of living has put many young people off marrying, buying a house, and having children. Experts are advising the government to relax the stringent immigration laws.

A Chinese road during rush hour

China, on the other hand, has had a population explosion to the extent that family size is restricted to one child. That is difficult to appreciate, considering the thousands of young children we encountered in the first few days here.

In Japan, very few cars on the road are more than three years old. In China, there are very few cars (per head).

Before commencing with my impressions of Asia in general and China in particular, I propose to cover my last impressions of Japan with a brief insight into Hong Kong.

Our final night in Japan, the Odyssey 2000 party went up in the world, *literally*. Our coach arrived at our hotel close to Osaka Airport in the dark, around 9 p.m. We were allocated two or three to a room, and having collected our room key, John and I made our way to the fourth floor, looking for room 561. Strange, we thought, as we could only locate conference rooms.

Returning to reception, we were told, "You are in room 61 on the forty-fifth floor." So it was back to one of the many high-speed lifts, and one of the best rooms we had on Odyssey. *This must be near the top,* I thought. But no, there were another eleven floors above ours with the restaurant at the top. As you can appreciate, the views we had by night and day were stunning, to say the least. We were advised that this hotel was, in fact, the second tallest building in Japan. So full marks to TK and A for the final night of luxury in Japan.

Greetings from Hong Kong

The following morning, we had a scheduled flight to Kuala Lumpur (one of the most modern and sophisticated airports we had yet passed through) en route to Hong Kong. We had thirty-six hours in which to experience the many delights which Hong Kong has to offer the first-time visitor.

The world's largest floating restaurant (Hong Kong)

Hong Kong must be one of the most densely populated regions in the world, with a total approaching seven million in the territory and almost two million on the island of Hong Kong. The island itself has some of the most expensive real estate in the world.

As most readers are probably aware, on 1 July 1997, Britain handed back to China the lease that it had held for ninety-nine years. The British and Chinese governments reached an agreement that Hong Kong and the New Territories would remain a special administrative zone of China's for fifty years. During this period, left-hand traffic, the currency, and the educational system would remain unaffected. Time will tell whether the Beijing government will honour the fifty-year agreement. Having said that, China would be ill advised to interfere too much with the newly acquired golden goose, since the bulk of all investments in China flow through Hong Kong. (The city has the world's largest concentration of banks.)

On Sunday, 15 October, the Odyssey cavalcade (complete with bicycles) departed from Hong Kong for the four-hour ferry ride to Zhaoqing. This was followed by a four-hour coach journey to the town of Wuzhou, from which we would resume our pedalling after an enforced break. The guidebooks describe this region as the Sensuous South. We shall see just how sensuous in my next update.

My previous update ended before my impressions of life in China. Life there is so different from anywhere else that we had so far gone in the world. I did also reflect on what life might have been like if democracy and capitalism had been allowed to flourish. I have since read that the state has eased its grip on economic activity to the extent that it now employs only 50 per cent of the working population. It is also encouraging foreign investment.

China is huge; likewise is its population, which is industrious and works hard to support its families. We saw men and women of all ages carrying large loads of goods on their bikes, motorcycles, and weird-looking three-wheel diesel trucks. The roads are congested with bicycles, motorcycles, and pedestrians. The majority of motor vehicles (and coaches) are commercial, most of which would fail a UK MOT test.

The standard of driving is very poor, and the right of way at a junction appears to go to the largest vehicle. This I had proved to me when a vehicle coming out of a turn on my right almost knocked me off my cycle. At home, I would have had the right of way—not so in China. Ironically, the truck in this incident had written on its side door, in English, "Never let an obstacle stand in your way."

We witnessed two road accidents in three days, both involving coaches. Two Odyssey riders narrowly missed the second, which included some fatalities, including children. Speaking of children, and on a more cheerful note, children in almost every country we travelled through took an interest in Odyssey 2000. But in China, we were astounded, almost embarrassed, by the interest and reception we got from the younger generation.

I will never forget seeing these happy, cheerful young children who lined the road in the thousands as we passed through each village and town. The amazing thing was that many of these children, as young as three years old, could speak English—not very much, I must admit. The first and most common greeting we got was "Hello," which was sometimes followed by "How are you?" And if you listened carefully, you may have heard a "Goodbye." Then one evening, as we stepped out of our hotel after supper, young autograph hunters besieged us.

Another aspect of life in China made me reconsider my diet in that, until we returned to Western culture, I decided to be vegetarian. While in Hong Kong, we were advised to avoid eating hot dogs in China. Some days later, I passed a butcher's shop and saw a man about to chop up a dog carcass. Snakes and numerous other animals we treat as pets are delicacies. It was not long before I went right off meat in Asia.

John. I did continue to eat meat when I thought it was well cooked. The only time I nearly followed Arthur into a vegetarian diet was when presented with a basket of day old chicks cooked in plum sauce. The chicks were eaten whole including the beak and feet. No one on the table would touch them so I consumed a number to make sure they didn't go to waste. I came to the conclusion that they were definitely an acquired taste, and not one I wished to develop.

So back to our itinerary, which took us to the towns of Yangshuo and Guilin, both of which are in the centre of China's second most popular tourist region, which attracts over three million visitors a year. On Monday, 16 October, Odyssey 2000 caused a minor sensation when we prepared to depart the town of Wuzhou. This town is not on the regular tourist route, so the sight of any Western travellers is unusual, to say the least. So, bearing in mind that all Chinese adults wear clothing which covers most of the body, seeing over two hundred cyclists wearing shorts and brightly coloured jerseys must have made us appear like aliens from outer space.

On the morning of our departure, a large crowd gathered outside our hotel as gear trucks were loaded and bikes prepared for the road (after two weeks in storage). One female member of the party, who had to replace an inner tube before starting, was assisted (in Chinese fashion) by at least fifteen local men of all ages. I'm not quite sure whether it was the inner tube being replaced or the young lady in shorts that was the centre of attraction.

For the next two weeks, a major addition to the Odyssey staff were local drivers, who were hired for our support vehicles and gear trucks. Visiting tourists are not allowed to drive on the road in China. Then, we also needed the services of an interpreter.

Another very welcome addition to the Odyssey staff at this point was a Dr Peter James (and his wife) from Seattle. A number of Odyssey riders were qualified medical folk and would assist in an emergency. But in recent months, people had expressed concern over the lack of medical staff, particularly as we passed through Asia, where local medical aid is very limited. On our second day in Hong Kong, John (my UK companion) happened to get into conversation with Dr Peter James and his wife at breakfast. This chat revealed that Peter and John had attended the same school at Hull in Yorkshire, Peter having immigrated to the USA in 1958. It is indeed a small world we live in.

John. Actually the school was in York .I didn't know Peter James at school but had a good chat with him when we met in China.

Find a Bike!

So back to our first day on the roads in China; on paper, we had a modest ninety-five kilometres to the town of Xindu, with a few rolling hills. At the end of the day, we all agreed that it had not been a normal ninety-five kilometres.

It was twenty kilometres into the ride that we encountered a fifty-kilometre stretch of our road which was under construction. China repairs its roads in a much different way than we are used to having our roads patched up in the West, where one stretch of road is repaired before work starts on the next. I'm not sure whether this happens nationwide in China, but on our fifty-kilometre stretch of road, we had small gangs of workers toiling (mainly by hand) on their own little bit of the road. It was a hot, dry day, so not only were we riding on long stretches of unmade road, but with every vehicle that passed us, a cloud of red dust would envelop us. So we were glad to get back on normal roads the following day.

John. One road we rode along had smart white line markings. On close examination the white line was seen to be made entirely from broken pottery i.e. broken plates, saucers etc. which were glued to the road with tar. We saw a gang of female workers cutting the grass beside one road. As far as I could see they were squatting down and cutting the grass with q pair of scissors only! They were making a very good job of it.

Four-wheel rural transportation

I think all of us in the West are well aware that the quality of life in China is way below that found in most of the Western world. In our travels this year, we had seen some depressed regions, but nothing to compare with what we were now travelling through. Life here was so different than it was in any other country we had so far been to this year. Communism in real time—that is China struggling to integrate into a shrinking world without losing control of the people or allowing Western ideals to influence its citizens, I wonder what life would be like there today if democracy and capitalism had been allowed to flourish.

Saturday, 21 October, was a layover day in the featureless city of Guilin, which has a population of 350,000. To see exactly what it is that attracts over three million visitors a year to the city's surrounding area, fifty Odyssey folk, including yours truly, decided to take a four-hour river cruise.

The cruise took us along the River Lijiang, where we saw at close quarters some strange limestone mountains, which we had seen from a distance for several days. It appears that nature laid the foundations of Guilin's present-day attraction over three hundred million years ago, when the region was underwater. Then, the water receded and exposed a limestone plateau, which over the years has eroded away. What remain are the strange karst peaks, which today rank among China's main tourist attractions. This all helped make our four-hour river cruise to Yangshuo a very memorable experience.

John. I had always thought the misty landscapes with lumpy hills that you see in Chinese watercolours were a figment of the artist's imagination. In fact they are a fair representation oh the karst scenery of South West China.

Another two days' riding took us to the town of Longsheng, where a rest day enabled us to visit another major attraction in this region. This time, we took a two-hour coach ride up into the mountains to view the famous Longji rice area and the Dragon's Backbone terraced fields, all of which were developed hundreds of years ago and still remain in active use.

We spent our final day and two nights in China in luxury at Nanning, which has a population of 650,000 and is the southernmost town in China. It is, in fact, just 160 kilometres from the border of Vietnam, the next country on our itinerary. The five-star Guangxi Nanning International Hotel had originally been booked for one night only, our last in China.

The previous night, at the end of day 300's 170-kilometre ride, we were due to stay at four different hotels in the small town of Binyang. This was normal in most of the smaller towns, which just could not accommodate the whole of Odyssey in one hotel. It appeared that the town of Binyang's total resources could not cope with such a large number of visitors in one go. Arising from this, after a shower and supper, the entire Odyssey cavalcade was taken by coach the eighty-six kilometres to Nanning, where we arrived around 9.30 p.m. on day 300 (26 October).

John. The drive in the dark was quite frightening, and we were glad to arrive in one piece..

The reception we received at the Gungxi Nanning Hotel surpassed anything we had experienced since the start of Odyssey. The hotel's main foyer was fully decorated with balloons and streamers and a large poster, which said, "We warmly welcome the excellent riders of Odyssey 2000", in red and white letters.

In addition, on our arrival at the hotel, our luggage was taken directly to our rooms whilst we were given a champagne reception. It had been a long day, with over a hundred-mile ride, followed by a fifty-four-mile coach trip with supper in between, so when my head hit the pillow around midnight, I was out for the count.

Before our next country, I have some final thoughts on our thirteen days in China—not long for such a huge country, but I have two words to describe the downside of my impressions, which are *pollution* and *poverty*. It has pollution in every possible form, in the exhaust fumes from every vehicle. Coal fires, both domestic and commercial, are contributing to the contamination. Rivers are polluted, and this gets worse close to urban areas. Sanitation is very poor in rural areas and not much better in urban locations.

In spite of the poverty and pollution, I found the Chinese to be friendly and industrious. Regrettably, the system still has both men and women working on the most menial (and, to me, soul-destroying) employment. Women in the country commonly cut grass along the roadside one blade at a time. Many of the road sweepers are female.

The tremendous reception given to the whole Odyssey 2000 party in China left a lasting impression on me. It was not uncommon to see a large group of locals (mainly children) centring their attention on an Odyssey rider changing an inner tube or having a snack. This became embarrassing at times, as I found to my cost one day when I stopped for a call of nature.

Yours truly saw not a soul in sight as I turned off the road into the privacy of a tree-lined lane. I had hardly dismounted my bike when a dozen smiling young children surrounded me. Then, I took a banana out of my bag and smiled back at them, and needless to say, I remounted my bike to look for another secluded spot.

John. This is the only Chinese symbol I learned. It means gents WC or washroom. These most certainly are for none but the brave.

Greetings from Vietnam!

We crossed the border into Vietnam at 16.40 on Sunday, 29 October. It took four hours by coach from our Nanning hotel to reach the border. It took another four hours to process the whole Odyssey party through the Chinese and Vietnamese immigration and customs. These two Communist countries are not easy to enter or exit at the best of times, let alone with 220-odd bicycles and bodies, and luggage, all of which went towards making it the longest border crossing this year.

Goodbye from China

At the Chinese border, we had to unload all luggage and cycles. We couldn't take any vehicles that had gone with us throughout China across the border; so new vehicles awaited us in Vietnam. Having been led out by the Chinese authorities, we then had to walk with our bikes and luggage through four hundred metres of no man's land to the Vietnamese crossing.

I had recently read that there had been moves to restore diplomatic relations (severed in '75 by the US) between the USA and Vietnam. I did not express this private thought, but I feared what effect the arrival of over two hundred American cyclists might have on the future of those talks. My fear was unfounded, because we were met with a welcome banner and given a label for our coach and luggage, which was taken from us.

So, having crossed into Vietnam, we were then faced with another five-hour coach journey to the capital city of Hanoi.

John. On this journey someone asked if wee would be stopping for a WC break.. Yes they said, we stop for 'Happy House'. I thought that was a really nice name for a toilet Ah, we said, but what if there are no Happy Houses? Well, they said, in that case we stop for Happy Trees!

When you consider that there have been (until recent times) territorial disputes between China and Vietnam, you will appreciate why 90 per cent of our five-hour journey to Hanoi was on unmade roads (another reason for not cycling). All of this went towards an uncomfortable introduction to Vietnam, in spite of the beautiful scenery. So our arrival at the Hanoi hotel at around 10 p.m. brought the welcome completion of a very long day. This left Monday, 30 October, to explore Hanoi.

Coping with the currency in the forty-plus countries we had visited this year had been a challenge, to say the least. It was not always possible to establish the rate of exchange in advance of my arrival. Italy and China were two particular challenges, but Vietnam (with the dong) I found to be the greatest challenge.

In Hanoi, before I could even locate a bank or find the exchange rate, a reliable source informed me that I would have to pay 14,500 dong for a small bottle of beer. Now, if you wish to find out how I became a millionaire in Vietnam, I can now reveal how I walked away from a Hanoi bank with a bulging wallet in local currency (the dong).

We were informed that the city only had one bank with an ATM, and that was five kilometres away. As my stock of US dollars and traveller's cheques was getting low, John and I felt that an early visit to the bank was advisable. We arrived at the bank by taxi before it was open. "This is not a problem," I confidently told John as I pointed to the two ATMs outside, one of which was in use. So John drew his cash with no problem and said that he would wait for me in the taxi.

I then inserted my Visa card only to be told that the PIN was incorrect. Having used this card *and number* since January, I was puzzled. So after two more unsuccessful attempts, I rejoined John in the waiting taxi and said I would cash a traveller's cheque at the hotel.

Later that day, we happened to pass the same bank, so I thought I would give the cash machine another try. This time, I walked away smiling and with a bulging wallet of notes in Vietnamese currency, to the value of 1.5 million dong. Yes, I was a millionaire, even if it did take four attempts. I trusted there would be no computer error when the withdrawal hit my account at home, because at twenty thousand dong to one pound sterling, I anticipated having drawn a modest seventy-five pounds.

Now, where was I before all that money went to my head? Ah yes, in Vietnam. So for the benefit of those who are not familiar with the geographical and political background to this beautiful country, this is my information.

We entered Vietnam in the extreme north from its Communist neighbour China. On the western border are Laos and Cambodia. The major attraction for visitors must be the 3,500-plus kilometres of the western South China Sea coast, along which the guidebooks say are many beautiful and untouched beaches. This I can confirm, as on our journey south, we did travel along this coast by train for several hours. In addition, there are caves, grottoes, and architecture to explore, if you have the time (which we did not).

Regrettably, the country and its people suffered turmoil and conflict from 1894 to 1954 when the French occupied it, and then again (as most will know) from 1963 to 1975, with the USA's unsuccessful attempt to prevent the Communist North Vietnam from its takeover of the democratic South Vietnam. Today, Vietnam remains a one-party state, and while some economic reform has occurred, there is no sign of this spreading to the political scene. However, after many years of stagnation, the economy is growing with recent offshore finds of oil and gas. Rice production has expanded to the extent that Vietnam, once an importer, is now the world's third largest exporter of rice after the USA and Thailand.

In spite of all of that, Vietnam is still a poor country. The United Nations estimates that 51 per cent of the population lives below the poverty line. It is hoped that economic development and foreign investment will continue to eliminate large-scale poverty. Happily, I found a similarity between the hard-working and friendly Chinese and the Vietnamese. I was also pleasantly surprised with the capital city of Hanoi.

Here are my thoughts on Hanoi, Hue (the early capital of Vietnam), and our thirty-hour train journey to South Vietnam, where I hoped to do some cycling. Hanoi is a city where I would like to have spent more than one day, which was all our schedule allowed. It is a city surrounded by water with many fine buildings and ultra-modern hotels.

As with any city and country with a history of colonial occupation (one hundred years by the French, ending in 1954), there are grim reminders of that period. One such reminder is the now-restored Hoa Lo Prison, which is considered a historic relic. The prison was built by the French in 1896 and was then the largest in Northern Indo-China. The official literature on the prison's grim historical record says that the French used it to imprison thousands of patriots and revolutionary fighters. Keeping prisoners in prison cells and chains, this harsh living and draconian custody actually turned the prison into a revolutionary school. The area was liberated in 1954, and from 1964 to 1973, part of the prison was used to detain American pilots who had been shot down while on bombing raids over North Vietnam.

While in Vietnam, one Odyssey wit quoted that only one thing compares with a night at the Hilton or the Sheraton Hotel, and that is a night of travel on a Vietnamese train with two hundred cyclists. This was an experience not to be missed (or repeated). In fact, we had not one but two nights on a Vietnamese train. Fortunately for us (and the tour organiser), they were split up with a layover day at the city of Hue, one-time capital of Vietnam.

There are three grades of travel on a Vietnamese train. There are wooden seats; wooden seats that are padded (and if you are lucky, they recline as well), which was our grade; and sleeping berths. The ultimate luxury is the squat toilet.

So why was our long journey south from Hanoi by train, anyway? This was not on the original itinerary but had been introduced partly as a result of the recent widespread flooding and to allow more time for biking in the south. The tour organisers also faced a problem with finding enough available adequate accommodation for 220 folk in one town. There were no camping facilities on the whole itinerary in Asia.

John. As Arthur says there was widespread flooding in Vietnam so I didn't take much notice at first of television pictures of flooding. However there was something familiar about the pictures and looking closely I saw the flooding was actually in Britain. Amazing to see flooding in Britain on TV whilst in well flooded Vietnam.

So on 31 October, we departed from the central station at Hanoi at 21.50. And we anticipated we would arrive at Hue at 14.40 the next day. Those who were awake during the daylight hours had an opportunity to see the (partly flooded) countryside in a more leisurely fashion than from our bike saddles.

The town of Hue, which was the twenty-four-hour break in our thirty hours of train travel, has five universities and a population of thirty thousand. About 49 per cent of the city's income comes from tourism. Just one four-hour tour will confirm why Hue is so popular with travellers, with its royal palaces, pagodas, historic building complex, and tradition of culture and art.

Royal Palace City of Hue

The final leg of our train journey south took us along the rugged coastline of the South China Sea to the resort of Nha Trang. From there, we were to commence our Vietnam biking experience.

This is my penultimate update on Vietnam, and I will dispatch it from Thailand when we arrive in Phuket by air on Thursday, 9 November.

Well, Odyssey 2000 had now been travelling for over 310 days through more than forty countries, and cycled 24,540 kilometres. During this period, we had seen a lot of the human race. However, I had no doubt that I had seen more of the human race in the last four weeks than in all the rest of the year put together. Particularly when passing through or leaving any large town in the morning, the roads are just one heaving mass of humanity. About 90 per cent of people are travelling on two wheels, another 8 per cent are on foot, and the rest are on four wheels. So I now have the solution to the UK's traffic problems (and I know I am preaching to the converted here). Yes, 90 per cent of the UK should commute or travel on two wheels.

Getting back to our two wheels, we set out from Nha Trang for the town of Da Lat, another popular tourist area with a perfect climate. It could be that this region's climate has something to do with its altitude. Yes, we did some serious climbing en route to Da Lat for approximately fifty kilometres. Our route took us through spectacular and mountainous terrain very reminiscent of Costa Rica.

John. Around this point we visited a village which had been in dispute with a neighbouring village. The local shaman was consulted and his solution was for the villagers to build a large, approximately 20 foot tall, concrete chicken between the two villages. This weird apparition was hollow and you could climb inside it. Apparently it worked and the dispute was settled. Maybe this approach should be considered by our politicians at home. If building concrete chickens solves disputes the technique has a lot going for it. In Britain we soon wouldn't be able to move for concrete chickens!

After a long and very hot day, we were rewarded with another layover day to relax and explore this area. Although there were a number of large hotels in Da Lat, the Odyssey party was split among three separate hotels.

On our departure from Da Lat two days later, I first met a very enterprising eight-year-old, who later turned out to be an orphan. We had an eight-hundred-metre walk from our hotel to collect our bikes at the host hotel. I must have looked in need of assistance, as I left the hotel carrying just my bar bag, my rack bag, three water bottles, and my helmet. I suddenly realised that someone or something had taken hold of my rack bag. Looking down, I saw what one could only describe as a cheerful, barefoot urchin.

Having been warned about vagrants and begging children, I smiled at the lad but hung on to my bag. After two hundred or so metres, the lad was still there and insisting that he could manage the bag on his own. So I relented and let him carry the bag; not sure whether this was a wise move, at the same time, I was prepared to retrieve it at short notice. We arrived at the host hotel intact with all my baggage, including our barefoot urchin, who I must admit seemed to know his way around.

Two days and 260 kilometres later, we arrived at the coastal resort of Phan Thiet for two very pleasant nights there. The following morning, I agreed to walk to the town with six of my companions. We had not gone more than one hundred metres from our hotel when we passed a small group of children playing. The next thing I knew, we were being followed, and looking round, I could not believe my eyes.

"John," I said, "we are being followed. Do you recognise who it is?" Yes, it was my little assistant bag carrier from Da Lat. Having said that, I was not really sure where he was from. Neither was I sure whether he had caring parents, as we were now 260 kilometres from where we had first seen him.

This marks my final report from Vietnam, transmission of which will be delayed. As anticipated, communication from Asia is patchy.

At the end of the last update, I told my story about the eight-year-old Vietnamese orphan. Lack of space prevented me from finishing that interlude and our last few days in Vietnam. I am sure that there must be many more sad cases like our youngster's, whose parents either died or abandoned them at an early age.

His name, we managed to establish, was Gole; at least this was how he pronounced it. No doubt the spelling was different. It was at the Vietnamese coastal resort of Phan Thiet that Gole had turned up, 260 kilometres from where we first met. It was a layover day, and six of my companions and I had agreed to walk to the town, market, and harbour. So we completed our walk with the help of our eight-year-old tour guide, who seemed to know his way around this town as well as the previous one. Whilst it was not easy to communicate with Gole, he appeared to know where we wanted to go. At one point, some of us wanted to purchase bottles of cold drinking water, so he took us from one shop to another until cold bottled water was found.

Later that evening, we went for a drink at the local golf club, and who should be there having a drink with some Odyssey folk but our young friend Gole. Three days later, we were at the Ho Chi Minh City Airport two hundred kilometres away, preparing for our flight to Thailand, when along came Gole to wish us all goodbye. The general feeling was that the lad would go a long way; more than one Odyssey person would have been happy to adopt him.

We spent our last two days in Vietnam in the country's largest and very historic city of Ho Chi Minh City, originally Saigon. The city has a population of seven million, 30 per cent of which is of Chinese origin. In fact, around fifty-four minority groups are found throughout the country.

In spite of the diesel fumes and continual honking of horns, which you seem to get from every vehicle in Vietnam and China, Vietnam has an atmosphere which is different from that of any other country we had so far visited. It is an experience just to stand on any street corner and watch the mass of vehicles (90 per cent of which is two-wheeled) weave in and out with no one giving way but no collisions.

John . In China the two wheeled traffic consisted of bicycles, but in Vietnam they were mostly lightweight motorcycles. At rush hour the most amazing motor cycle traffic jams developed. Just watching the traffic was a great spectator sport.

Our final day in Ho Chi Minh City included the usual guided tour. On it, we took in the Independence Palace (where Vietnam was officially reunified) as well as the War Remnants Museum, which highlights the tragedy (on both sides) of the war with the USA.

There will be some delay in dispatching this update and future emails.

Greetings from the Kingdom of Thailand (formerly Siam), which has a Tesco and a Boots, and where we were back to cycling on the right (left) side of the road. Yes, we were still very much in Asia, but in a country with some Western influence. With Thailand the next country on the Odyssey 2000 itinerary, our two-hour flight from Vietnam took us to the beautiful island of Phuket.

Thailand was a new country for me, and my impression was that Phuket in particular and Thailand in general was a place one could return to (one day). As the brochure describes it, the island of Phuket is for the discerning international traveller; set in the shimmering Andaman Sea, it is the perfect year-round destination. It is a place to linger, but one day was our limit before getting back on the bikes for the seven days' ride south for Malaysia.

So what is so special about the island of Phuket? Unlike other major tourist attractions, it was not discovered as a holiday destination until the late 1960s. Then, only a few adventurous backpackers discovered it. The choice of things to see and do in Phuket was so wide that we found it difficult to decide with just one day at our disposal. So a large number of Odyssey folk selected a whole-day tour to Phang Nga.

This required a coach journey to the mainland at the north-east of the island. We then took a speedboat tour, which took us through a maze of mangroves, where the driver demonstrated his skills by weaving in and out of the trees. We then visited the "James Bond island," which is now a national park. Some scenes from the movie *The Man with the Golden Gun* were filmed here. Judging by the number of visitors to this island and subsequent photographs, this could be the most famous tiny island around Phuket.

Our lunch destination was a stilted fishing village with numerous eating houses. Our boat was moored to the wharf, and we entered the open seafood restaurant via a rickety gangplank. Having eaten our lunch of crab, squid, fish, chicken, and prawns with generous helpings of rice, we departed for the final part of the tour: an elephant trek.

It appears that the elephant population in Thailand has dropped from one hundred thousand to five thousand over the past one hundred years. This is partly due to the fact that logging was officially banned in the '80s, putting many elephants in the ranks of the unemployed. Regrettably, some elephants still work illegally in the timber industry, where they are treated badly, some fed amphetamines to increase their workload.

In 1998 an organisation called the Elephant Help Project was set up in Phuket. The Thailand tourism authority, plus other commercial bodies and banks, sponsor it. Arising from this organisation's work, the fifteen elephants on Phuket in 1994 have now increased to 172, with 27 trekking companies. This all means that the elephants are now employed and well cared for.

Our one-hour elephant trek through the jungle was a pleasant climax to our full-day tour. The final treat came from one talented elephant, who gave us a tune on a mouth organ and then gave one brave volunteer, who laid on the ground, a back massage with one of the elephant's front feet.

As anticipated, email and phone communication from Asia has not been easy or cheap, hence the delay since the last update. However, there are just twelve days of cycling left in Asia that I have to report on—six days each in Thailand and Malaysia.

As indicated in the last report, Thailand is a country of discovery. This was so obvious from my first brief visit that I *will* come back, and I was even in danger of falling in love with the country. Historically speaking, Thailand is the only country in South East Asia that has not been subjected to any long-term foreign domination. It also has a constitutional monarchy, with the present respected monarch being the longest reigning monarch in Thai and world history.

In spite of the few tropical storms and the humidity, our last two weeks in Asia were the most memorable days of riding we had this year. Prior to our arrival in the area, the group had some feelings of apprehension over accommodation, food, and our itinerary in general. But as we progressed from China into Vietnam, then into Thailand and Malaysia, our fears and concerns diminished. The quality of our accommodation improved as we progressed; the food, and especially the friendly welcome we received, did likewise.

Three days later, we arrived at our final stop in Thailand, the coastal town of Narathiwat. It was here that the local bicycle club welcomed Odyssey 2000 and jerseys were exchanged. Later that evening, we were treated to local entertainment by Thai dancers and musicians. This was followed by a welcome speech from the town mayor and tourist board.

On day 322 (17 November), after just forty kilometres, we arrived at the short ferry crossing, which took us across the border and into Malaysia. This was a short day, with a total of seventy kilometres to the coastal town of Kota Bharu.

What no Odyssey rider was prepared for was the reception we received on our arrival in Malaysia and for the remaining six days. As we cycled off the ferry, up to the terminal and immigration office, we saw a large banner hanging across the road. The banner read as follows: "A very warm welcome to Odyssey 2000 from the people of Malaysia." We had not experienced something like this on any other border crossing this year.

Whenever Odyssey entered or exited a country, it always had a queue at immigration and customs. The length and speed of the line varied depending on the country and how we arrived. In this case, there was a ferry every hour throughout the day, so our crossing was spread over several hours; there were around forty riders on our ferry. The wait at the immigration window was not too long, but beyond that was another line.

"What's the holdup this time?" we asked.

The answer "We can't move till we are all here because we have a police escort" came back.

As we only had thirty-five kilometres to ride to our hotel, we assumed there was some diversion or road construction. This was not the case; at least twelve motorcycle police escorted the party of forty-odd riders all the way to our hotel at Kota Bharu. We had no need to refer to our route sheet; a motorcycle policeman was at every junction, holding up the traffic and waving us through. This treatment was special, to say the least, and made us feel like royalty or the Tour de France peloton.

John. Arthur you are not kidding! At one hotel we went into dinner walking on a red carpet whilst young ladies threw scented petals over us and waved artificial palm trees made of tinsel at us! Wow! I've never experienced anything like that before, it was like something dreamed up by Hollywood.

The next few days, our route followed the 225-kilometre coastline south through the state of Terengganu. This is an area endowed with a wealth of natural and charming landscapes. It has miles and miles of white sandy beaches; lush, virgin tropical jungle; and quaint fishing villages. And offshore are several exotic islands to explore (for those who have the time). Unfortunately, the weather was not as kind as the scenery. We arrived at the height of the rainy season; at least it was warm rain.

John. This was the only part of Odyssey where I welcomed the rain which was frequent and heavy. When it rained there was some relief from the muggy heat. The constant damp rotted my track mitts (cycling gloves) and they just fell apart.

To conclude our final days in Malaysia—a country which gave us a far greater welcome than any other we had visited—we passed through the state capital of Kuala Terengganu on our third day in the Malaysian state of Terengganu (population one million). It was mid-morning and just fifty kilometres into the day. It was also raining hard, and we had been warned to expect some delay that morning. We had no indication of what the delay might be, but as we came into town, there was a police roadblock for all traffic except Odyssey riders, who were waved through.

Two hundred metres on, a band was playing with a large marquee on either side of the road. In one open tent, a large group of Odyssey riders tucked into a buffet with coconuts and fruit juice. In the other marquee were a dozen official-looking folk, press and TV cameras, and the Odyssey tour organiser. It soon became evident that this was an official welcome to Terengganu by the state governor and the tourism board. After several welcome speeches, a presentation was made, and the official party crossed the road (complete with umbrellas) to meet individual riders. All on Odyssey 2000 would remember the whole of our Asia itinerary—in particular the happy, cheering children—for a long time to come.

Two days later, on 24 November (day 329), we took the forty-five-minute ferry ride into Singapore and ended stage 12 with fond memories of Asia in general but of Malaysia in particular. The daily route guide (DRG) for that day indicated the itinerary statistics for the total stage in kilometres (1,597) and the total trip in kilometres (26,146 a/f 1 January). Only five folk had ridden every kilometre; yours truly could claim approximately twenty-four thousand.

At this point in our year long epic bike ride, all participants who had already invested a large chunk of their personal savings faced a difficult decision. For some weeks, there had been doubts over the remaining thirty-seven days of this bike ride of a lifetime. We had been told in October that due to fuel cost increases since the Odyssey budget had been set seven years prior, a surcharge of three thousand US dollars per person would have to be levied to those who wanted to complete the itinerary.

Following several meetings when various options were put forward and considered, there was no change for those wishing to complete the itinerary. Having spent eight weeks cycle touring in New Zealand three years before, I could not justify spending three thousand dollars to return for twenty-one days, beautiful as it was.

Approximately sixty-five folk paid up and departed for Christchurch from Singapore on 26 November. A similar number decided to call it a day and head for home, while some decided to hang on in Asia. Having made plans based on our finish in LA on 31 December, I and my fellow UK rider, John, decided on another option, which the Odyssey organisers made available. For the sum of $1,200, we would rejoin the Odyssey party in Hawaii on 17 December for the final two weeks so we could join the finish in California. This figure included our flight from Singapore to Hawaii.

So our flight to Hawaii was booked for 10 December. And with two weeks in Singapore and one week in Hawaii to spare, we came to be on the Getaway Island of Bintan (Indonesia), just a fifty-minute ferry ride from Singapore and approximately forty miles north of the equator. Now was the time to reflect on cycling over the Andes in February and the Pyrenees in April, *both in a blizzard*, whilst I languished in the South China Sea for two weeks.

Season's greetings from Kona on the Big Island of Hawaii. I dispatched my last update from the island of Bintan in the South China Sea. Since then, yours truly has been taking a break, with just three days on the bike.

On 16 December, we reunited with the Odyssey party (around sixty-five people) who flew in from New Zealand late on 15 December. We were now into the final fourteen days of this epic bike ride.

I'm not quite sure how many more updates it is going to take before I give this machine a break. However, I need to put some reflections on the past three weeks into print. The first indicates just how small this planet Earth really is. At the Bintan Island hotel check-in at the end of November, a lady of Eastern origin recognised one of our Odyssey ID tags and approached John and me. "Yes," we said to her query, "we are part of Odyssey 2000."

"Well," said the lady, "I met you all in Stockholm, where I now live, back in August. I know two of your party. I originate from Singapore, and we are here on vacation."

Then one day last week, we were cycling on the island of Kauai here in Hawaii when a car went past and pulled over. Winding down his window, the American driver said, "Are you with Odyssey 2000?"

"Yes," replied John. It appeared that the couple in the car had been on a cycling holiday in China at the same time and in the same location as us.

To change the subject, on the day before we left Singapore for Hawaii, yours truly was reading the *Singapore Straits Times* dated 9 December. In it, I read an article which made me smile. It covered a topic which any world traveller would be well equipped to write about: public toilets around the world. For the benefit of those readers who may be interested, I will pick out the main points of the news item that caught my eye. The headline was as follows: "Beijing's Dirty Toilets to Get a Good Scrub". The article continued, "In a bid to host the 2008 Olympic Games, the Chinese capital is spending $37 million to upgrade public lavatories in tourist spots."

So, Beijing wouldn't be smelly anymore. The Chinese capital was going to clean up its notoriously foul public toilets as part of its bid to host the 2008 Olympic Games. Beijing appeared to have 452 toilets in its main tourist spots, of which tourists currently used only 60. The article said all of them *must* be renovated in the next two years.

So, to continue, on 10 December, John and yours truly presented ourselves at the China Air check-in counter of Singapore Airport en route to Honolulu. We were looking forward to a return to Western culture in the USA (and the final two weeks of Odyssey 2000), but Uncle Sam had other ideas. Our return to the USA (our third in twelve months) was not going to be quite that easy, as we found out when we presented ourselves at the check-in counter. A familiar question was put to us: "When are you planning to leave the USA? And do you have your onward tickets?" (like "Nice to see you, but when are you leaving?"). When we gave a negative answer to the last question, it appeared to ring alarms, with the comment "If we allow you onto the plane without your onward tickets, it is very likely that the US immigration authorities will put you on the next plane back to Singapore."

So feeling like a couple of refugees, we got on the phone to Tony at Number 10, who promised to ring Bill before he left the White House. Then, within the hour, we had our boarding tickets.

Now the *truth*. "Well," we said meekly to the check-in lady, "we do have onward tickets, but they are with our travel agent in Los Angeles."

She politely told us this was not any help. "You must have an onward ticket in your possession," she said.

So after further consultation and a telex with China Air in Honolulu, we were advised the only way around the problem was for us to buy an open return ticket from Honolulu to Singapore. "That will cost you 1,200 Singapore dollars each," we were told. So let that be a lesson to any would-be UK travellers planning to visit Uncle Sam, visa waiver or not.

Then, to complicate and confuse your two weary travellers even more, we left Singapore at 15.00 hours on 10 December. And after two flights of five and eight hours, changing planes in Taiwan, we arrived at Honolulu just two hours before we had left Singapore (13.00 hours on 10 December), all thanks to the international dateline.

So we were at long last back in the United States, and very impressed we were with the speed and efficiency with which we went through customs and immigration, who did not even ask to see the China Air return ticket in my hand. Within ninety minutes, we were on an inter-island flight to the Garden Island of Kauai, where I had a problem coping with ten hours of sunshine per day, in the warmest part of the USA. The only consolation was to think of England in December.

John. Whilst in Honolulu we managed to get a refund from China Air for the unused tickets we had bought merely to satisfy the requirement to be in physical possession of an onward air ticket (as we had finally received the original tickets). This was issued without a quibble so I guess the China Air Office in downtown Honolulu was used to the procedure.

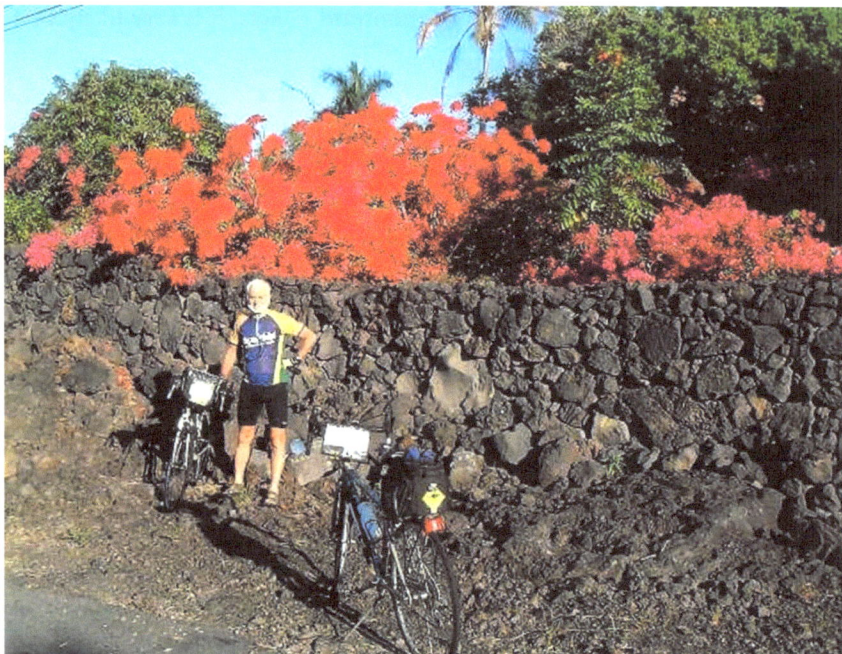

My last update ended around 10 December with our arrival in Hawaii from Singapore. You will recall that John and I took a twenty-one-day break from Odyssey 2000 while they were in New Zealand. We planned to rejoin them in Hawaii on 17 December for the final two weeks leading to Los Angeles. This gave us seven days in Hawaii before the Odyssey party arrived from New Zealand. We spent that period on the island of Kauai, one of the eight inhabited islands which make up the Hawaiian archipelago. It is also the oldest and westernmost of the inhabited islands. There are, in fact, over 130 islands.

So why did the Odyssey 2000 organisers select Hawaii for us to spend Christmas—a fitting prelude to our finale in California? Well, the fact that a large number of humpback whales are prepared to travel over 3,500 miles from Alaska to Hawaii in order to breed in the warm Pacific waters every December has nothing to do with Odyssey 2000. However, I guess if Hawaii is good enough for two-thirds of the North Pacific whale population, it must have been good enough for the survivors of Odyssey 2000.

John. I hadn't realised until too late that we would have a few days over Christmas to spare in Hawaii. Had I known this Celia my wife could have flown out to join us for a few days. She had previously come out to Cordoba in Spain, Amsterdam in the Netherlands, and to Burbank California for the beginning and end of Odyssey. Still I did manage to phone home, although because of the time difference I had to get up at 2.30 a.m. to do so.

I say *survivors* simply because when we had arrived in Singapore from Asia at the end of November, the group had approximately two hundred riders. When we met up with the party in Honolulu on 16 December, there were sixty-five riders including ourselves. Numerous factors contributed to the departure of such a large number, but the major reason was most likely the three-thousand-dollar surcharge imposed by the tour organiser.

For the benefit of some folks at home, maybe I should at this stage provide a little historical and geographical background to this very remote group of islands in the Pacific Ocean. The islands that make up Hawaii were born over forty million years ago from a volcanic eruption on the ocean bed. Hawaii is also the most remote land mass on earth, being 2,600 miles from the West Coast of the USA and 3,800 miles from Japan. In spite of the fact that one of the first white men to set foot here was the British explorer Captain James Cook in 1778, Hawaii is part of the USA and became a state on 12 March 1959. The only visible links with the UK today is the plot of land owned by the UK marking the spot where Captain Cook was killed, and the Hawaiian flag, which includes the Union Jack.

So our reunion with the Odyssey party took place on 16 December in Honolulu. The following day, we flew to the Big Island of Hawaii for five days of biking (and camping) around the island. This would be followed by three days to celebrate Christmas at the Kona resort on the south of the island.

The outcome of those few days on the Big Island together, with our return to California for the final two days and 120 miles of this epic bike ride, will be found in my final update.

New Year's greetings from California

This is where it all started; just 362 days ago, we crossed the border from California to Mexico. Since then, we had crossed many frontiers, and yours truly had written fifty-one updates. The fact that this is number 52, in the final week, is pure coincidence. We arrived back in California at Los Angeles International Airport at around 4 p.m. local time on Friday, 29 December (day 364). A 160-mile drive to San Diego would then commence the final two days cycling back to Los Angeles.

Before I comment on those two days, I have some notes which I have carried over from our last week in Hawaii that I was unable to cover in the last update.

We arrived on the largest and easternmost Hawaiian island on 17 December. It is commonly known as the *Big Island* because the seven other inhabited islands would fit into it. That is my theory, anyway. The Big Island is also the youngest of the Hawaiian Islands; it is made up of five volcanoes. Scientists estimate that it rose from the sea around half a million years ago. The highest volcano, Mauna Kea, rises nearly fourteen thousand feet above sea level. If measured from the base on the sea floor, Mauna Kea reaches up almost thirty-two thousand feet, making it the highest mountain on Earth.

So our pre-Xmas schedule for the sixty-five survivors of Odyssey 2000 was going to be a five-day camping ride around the island. On reflection, I think there was a move afoot to reduce our numbers even more before the festivities began.

After almost three weeks off the bike, the ride around the Big Island was for me (and many of my younger companions) a personal challenge. This became more so on the second day, when we climbed a modest four thousand feet into a headwind that turned to rain as we reached the summit. At this point, our DRG included an invitation (for those who were interested) to take a ten-mile detour around the island's only active volcano. In view of the poor visibility and rain, I decided to give the volcano a miss. I was then rewarded with a twenty-mile descent to the town of Hilo, and within five miles, we rode out of the rain and into clear blue skies and warm sunshine.

Two days later, we were faced with an eighty-mile ride. This route took us a very scenic, coastal route towards Onomea Bay. The destination on this day was on the north of the island of Hawaii, but like most of the islands, it has a wet side and a hilly side to contend with. The wet side gave us twenty miles of riding in the warm rain. Then we turned inland and towards the dry side, but just to make it a challenge, we had another four-thousand-foot climb, and into a headwind again.

On 23 December, we arrived back at the Kona resort on the south of the island, where we spent two very pleasant days relaxing in the sunshine. Then on Boxing Day, we flew to the neighbouring island of Maui for two nights. This was to be Odyssey 2000's final fling in Hawaii before our return to California. I was now beginning to appreciate why the islands of Hawaii attract seven million visitors per year.

I was hoping that this would be my last update, but there will be one more, as our last two weeks of Odyssey have been hectic.

The last update ended with our final fling in Hawaii, with two days on the island of Maui. Each of these islands has its own special charm, and Maui is no exception. Maui's natural beauty is the result of its explosive creation. A large chunk of that natural beauty was preserved for all time when the federal government created Haleakala National Park. This national park may have been the reason for our visit to Maui. Or was it some people's urge to cycle (climb) another mountain?

So on 28 December, we returned to Honolulu on the island of O'ahu in preparation for our five-hour flight to LA the next day. This gave us an opportunity to briefly visit Honolulu. This is where it all happens, on the world-famous Waikiki Beach and in the city of Honolulu, the most international city in the USA. Many TV shows and movies have enhanced the fame of this location.

For me, the most memorable and moving experience of the few hours spent in Honolulu was my visit to Pearl Harbor. Most readers will know why Pearl Harbor is now a historic site, but I found it an awesome place to visit. It was here, on 7 December 1941, that World War II began for the USA. In the early hours of Sunday, 7 December 1941, a massive air and sea attack on Pearl Harbour by the Japanese took many lives. It destroyed many US battleships lined up in the harbour. The principal victim was the USS *Arizona* and her 1,177-person crew, who lost their lives on that fatal day. The area is now a ten-acre cultural site, museum, and memorial.

Whilst many of the sunken ships were raised or removed, the USS *Arizona* has been left as a permanent memorial and resting place for her crew. Now, a 184-foot-long memorial, which spans the sunken battleship, can be clearly seen just below the surface. This memorial is also a shrine containing the names of those who died.

As I was only nine years of age when the USA declared war on Japan, I found our visit to Pearl Harbor the most moving experience this year. It was even more ironic when I thought back to our last day in Japan, 10 October, when I visited Peace Memorial Park in Hiroshima, where World War II came to an end.

This is where I must end this update, so if you really wish to see this project through to the finish, look out for my final report. That will be the final update before putting my cycle into storage and going into hibernation for a short period.

We arrived back in the mainland USA on 29 December, where it had all begun. A number of riders who left the tour at Singapore in November rejoined the group for the last two days, taking our number to approximately eighty. A large following in the USA and around the world had been monitoring the ups and downs of Odyssey 2000 via many websites. That plus the local media meant that folks in California and beyond knew who we were, where we had been, and where we were heading.

Regrettably, in spite of the party's buoyant mood, two female riders were admitted to hospital during those two final days. The first was brought to the ground by a skateboard, which ran into her front wheel and rendered her unconscious. The other female admitted to hospital was suffering from altitude sickness; this problem arose in Hawaii when a number of folk climbed the ten-thousand-foot volcanoes on the island of Maui. Once out of hospital, this rider had instructions to take a complete rest.

The route we took north followed the Pacific Coast Highway with an overnight stop at San Juan Capistrano. Our route on both days took us along popular bike trails and through national parks.

The Hilton Hotel in Burbank, on the outskirts of LA, was our final destination and resting place on 31 December. At 3.22 p.m. that day, I arrived at the Hilton with a party of eight companions; there, a group of well-wishers greeted us. I could not comprehend that it was actually all over. My feelings were difficult to describe—relief? Satisfaction? Then, what would come next?

The end. Now what?

John. Finished!! Celia was there to welcome us. Riding in the Tournament of Roses Parade next day we had learned from our previous experience and wore adequate clothing. Our formation was as ragged as before but even with our diminished numbers we still made quite an impressive sight. It had been a pretty memorable year. My thanks to Arthur for his company and to all the Odyssey staff and riders for the greatest experience of my life.

However, it was *not* all over yet. Dinner was at 7.30, followed by the usual speeches and celebrations till midnight; that is, for those still on their feet. People voiced admiration for the five individuals (including one female) who had cycled every mile of the itinerary. The last day's DRG indicated a total distance covered of 28,635 kilometres. My personal mileage was slightly less, having missed out on New Zealand, Ireland, and Scotland.

New Year's Day breakfast occurred at 5 a.m. As a result, some of us decided that the New Year would have to arrive without us.

Why was breakfast at that hour when Odyssey was over? you may ask. You may recall that last year, on 1 January, we were invited to lead the famous Tournament of Roses Parade, an annual extravaganza that has been running for 112 years and that takes place over a five-mile route in Pasadena and has a different theme each year. This invitation was repeated for 2001; and this year, the theme was the "Fabric of America".

Rose Parade (Pasadena)

1 January 2001

The event was listed in *TV Guide* as follows: "Starting at 8 a.m. the parade will include 24 marching bands, 26 equestrian units, and 52 floats all of which will illustrate the theme for 2001. There will also be a parachute drop by the US Army Golden Knights Team, and the return of the Odyssey 2000 cyclists from their year long trek around the world."

This was our final moment of glory, to be cheered by one million people who lined the five-mile route.

Final photo call

I now look forward to having a short break and catching up with my family. I then hope to make contact with all you good folk who have supported my efforts for the National Society for the Prevention of Cruelty to Children.

Happy New Year to you all.

Arthur Benbow,

Globe-Trotting Pensioner

Lightning Source UK Ltd.
Milton Keynes UK
UKHW052342030420
361323UK00002B/7